A M

30
FOR
30

THE WRITINGS BEHIND THE WALL:

A JOURNAL OF JENNIFER ROAD DETENTION CENTER

Darren Smith

30 for 30
The Writings Behind the Wall:
A Journal of Jennifer Road Detention Center

Published by
Kingdom Publishing, LLC
Odenton, Maryland U.S.A.

Printed in the U.S.A.

LCCN: 2020906526

ISBN: 978-1-947741-53-9 (Paperback)

ISBN: 978-1-947741-54-6 (eBook)

Foreword

"You have to do better Mr. Smith. You have a master's degree. You shouldn't be in here," the Case Manager exclaimed. I smiled politely and walked back to my cell. She was right though. Out of all the places, the Jennifer Road Detention Center (JRDC) in Annapolis, MD was the last place where I'd ever thought I'd find myself. Yet, here I was.

Now, for a brief synopsis as to how I arrived at this point. On the early morning of March 17th, 2018, I was arrested and charged with driving under the influence (DUI). I spent the remainder of 2018 going back and forth to court for this offense, as court dates would continue to get postponed and rescheduled.

As this case continued to hang over my head, I was also placed on administrative leave from my job in December of 2018 for an incident in which, unbeknownst to me, I violated an agency policy. This incident was indirectly related to this charge. My employer, DC Government Child and Family Services Agency (CFSA), submitted a request for my termination to DC Government Human Resources (DCHR). This request could either be approved by a hearing officer at DCHR, in which case I'd be terminated, denied, or thrown out altogether, both of the latter meaning I'd be reinstated. The final decision, regardless of the selection, would take time to reach, as the request still had to go through several levels of approval before anything was officially carried out. During this process, I was still being paid, but was not allowed to report to work until I received word of the final decision. Along with potentially facing jail time, my livelihood was now also suddenly at stake.

On March 6th, 2019, nearly a year from the date I was originally charged, I was convicted and sentenced to 60 days in jail, along with 1 year of supervised probation for which there were a host of other stipulations. The judge gave me until March 15th to turn myself in. This allowed me time to ensure that my personal affairs were in order prior to beginning my sentence.

My entire life, my mother has always told me that I am very insightful, and I maintain those same sentiments. Because of this, I know that there is essentially nothing about my lifestyle that would warrant me having to spend time in jail. I'm educated, have a good job, do not use drugs or involve myself in any criminal activity. I avoid drama in all ways possible, pay my taxes and bills in a timely manner, try to keep myself surrounded by good people, and am personable and respectful to others. So, in reference to the Case Manager's comment, no one recognizes the truth that lies within her statement more than me. I knew this prior to being here, and even more so upon my arrival, and now having to experience firsthand. But I cannot turn back the hands of time. I was here, rightfully being held accountable for a poor decision I had made.

So, as a way to make good use of my time, I figure I'd to use this opportunity to provide a glimpse into what life was like for me on a day-to-day basis while behind the wall. This memoir is based off of a daily journal I maintained during my brief stay in jail. I documented, as best I could, everything that happened to me each day while incarcerated, including the meals I ate, my daily interactions, the books and stories I read, my job and the duties it entailed, and any crazy experiences I encountered. Once released, I expanded on some of the entries to include my own personal thoughts and analysis. However, it all stems directly from the time that I spent in JRDC.

My hope is that this memoir about my time spent here, although an extremely short stint, will provide a deeper insight into what being incarcerated is like for those (like myself, prior to this) whose lives are so far removed from such an experience. Most importantly, I hope that in some way my words will inspire, and help someone else along the way that may find themselves in a similar predicament.

Receiving and Processing

Friday, March 15th, 2019. It was a little after 5pm.

"Call me as soon as they let you to use the phone," my mother said to me while we stood in front of the metal detector door in the front lobby. Before we parted ways, she gave me a hug, holding me as tight as she could. Then, speaking closely in my ear, in a voice that was struggling to hold back tears, said, "Jesus will protect you." "I know Ma," I replied. The correctional officer (CO) then escorted me back into the receiving wing of the jail, where each inmate must come once they arrive to go through processing. My stint here at JRDC officially starts now.

Once in processing, the first thing I had to do was turn over my property for them to retain until my release: IPhone XS Max, headphones, keys, wallet and $71 cash (which I told the officers was to be put on my commissary), 2 bracelets, and an extra pair of contacts. I informed them that I wear contacts everyday, so I was allowed to keep the contact case that I place them in at night before I go to sleep. If there's one place I want to make sure that I'm able to clearly see all that's around me throughout the day, it's in here. All of my belongings were placed in a small plastic bag and sealed shut.

Next, I had to get searched and changed. I was given a plain, dark green two-piece jail suit, and a pair of orange/black netted slip-on shoes without shoestrings. A CO then led me into a separate shower room. I was instructed to take off all of my clothes. Once naked, further instructions came. "Lift up your sack," the CO directed. I obliged. "OK. Now turn around, squat, and cough." I did as instructed, and then put on the jump suit I was issued. I then took a picture that would be used for my jail ID (JID) and was issued my JID number: 1474625. I'll end up becoming very familiar with this number, as

I'll have to use it each time I need to make a call while here. Next, I sat at a kiosk window for an intake interview by a female worker from the opposite side of the glass. She asked a number of preliminary questions (name, age address, emergency contact, etc.). Some other questions were also asked, I'm assuming, to gain better insight into what type of inmate I would be, or if extra safety precautions were needed for me during my stay.

"Are you a member of a gang?"
"No, ma'am."
"Do you feel like you'd want to hurt yourself?"
"No, ma'am."
"Straight, gay, transgender?"
"Straight."

After the brief intake interview, I was fingerprinted. Next, I was seen by the female nurse in the medical room of the receiving unit to wrap up the intake process. She was pleasant. She asked me some general questions regarding my health (whether or not I smoked, if I had any allergies, etc.), and then gave me a Tuberculosis shot in the inside of my left forearm, the results of which she said would be checked within a few days. I initially thought that the intake process would take forever, but it only took about 10-15 minutes, as I was the only person who needed to be processed at the time. Next, I was told that I could make a phone call.

I was allowed to make a toll-free call prior to being placed in one of the holding cells in the receiving unit. I called Moms to let her know that I was fine and that processing didn't take long at all. I could sense that hearing my voice so shortly after leaving gave her some sense of relief. After the call, I went into a holding cell (the "bullpen") where 2 other inmates had already been sitting and waiting.

On top of already feeling stupid and embarrassed for being in here altogether, this is where I began to feel somewhat apprehensive. Shit, there's no need to front. I was scared. I believe that walking into the unknown is something that customarily unmasks this type of feeling in us all. It's only natural for humans to feel nervous, anxious, and even fearful about going into a situation that you yourself have never experienced or know little to nothing about. But it is heightened when one is about to embark on an experience that is exclusively associated with being negative. Whether it be from the stories I've heard from others who've been jailed/incarcerated, to the way its been portrayed through music, books, TV and media, to the historical implications that it's had for black and brown men specifically, I've only known it as a place with which I've never wanted to be personally associated.

It was a little cold in the bullpen. I spoke a little with the guys who had already been sitting there. After about an hour, all 3 of us were called to be escorted back to a unit. Before being taken back, we each were issued a netted laundry bag full of supplies and toiletries that we were to use during our stay. The bag's contents:

- 1 Carolina blue blanket
- 2 Navy blue sheets
- Light orange rubber shower shoes
- 1 extra green jump suit
- 3 pieces of loose-leaf paper, short pencil, & 2 mailing envelopes
- 1 Navy blue hand towel
- 1 Navy blue washcloth

- Red windbreaker button up jacket (only issued from October thru April)
- 1 plastic toiletry bag ("Fresh Scent" gel deodorant, toothbrush and toothpaste, comb, 3-in-1 shower, shave, & shampoo gel. All travel size)
- 1 Orange plastic cup
- 1 yellow inmate orientation booklet

The intake process was officially over. We each took our designated laundry bags off of the counter and were led back into the unit. I am now the property of Anne Arundel County, an official inmate at JRDC. This would be my home for the next 2 months, as sentenced to me by a judge in court a week and a half ago.

A-1

With my netted laundry bag full of personal items tossed over my shoulder, the CO finally led us out of the receiving area and into unit A-1, the first stop during my stay. A-1 is usually the first stop for anyone (males) that is doing a stint at JRDC. It consists of a rather large dayroom with circular tables sitting throughout, chairs stacked along one side of the room, one TV, 3 sizeable showers right by the entrance, and 4 phones lined up beside each other on the front wall, behind where the TV is located. There are two floors of cells along the outside of the dayroom, and steps on each side of the dayroom to get from one level to the next. However, the 2nd floor cells were not being used. Once I entered A-1, I was told, along with one of the other men with whom I was waiting in receiving, that we both would be staying together in cell A-15.

A-1 is considered the "holding unit" area for everyone who does time at JRDC, prior to being moved to an actual "housing unit". Meaning, A-1 is only a temporary stay. If you're an inmate that's already been sentenced like myself, or an inmate awaiting trial, where you will eventually be housed once leaving A-1 depends upon the classification you receive.

So, here's how it works. Within the first few days to a week of you being on the A-1 tier, 1 of 2 things will occur. If you're a pretrial inmate, you will have a bail review hearing to determine whether or not you can be released, and under what conditions. If you have already been sentenced, or you're a pretrial inmate that's already been denied bail and must sit in jail until your court date, then you will be seen by a Case Manager. The Case Manager will assess the seriousness of your current charge, your criminal history, and other factors to determine what classification/rating you will receive. Your rating, which will be either minimum, medium, or maximum, determines which unit you will be housed in once you leave A-1, and what restrictions you'll have in regards to movement throughout the jail and the programs in which you can participate.

Upon my arrival to A-1, I quickly realized that it was the least desirable unit to be amongst all of the inmates during one's stay at JRDC. During the week, the dayroom of A-1 is where all of the bail reviews are held for every inmate (male and female) in the jail. Bail reviews begin around 8:30am and go until the late afternoon/early evening. During this time, all of the A-1 inmates are locked in their cells. We are allowed out for one hour in the morning, from 7:30am until 8:30am, then after this, locked away until 6pm. There is no access to the TV or phones until 6pm when they allow us out into the dayroom again. Then, once allowed out, the process to access the phone ensues.

Being that A-1 locks in at 10pm, that leaves only 4 hours in the evening for the entire unit, which can be anywhere from 25-40 people at a time, to watch a little TV, but most importantly, use the phones. Phone calls last for only 20 minutes, but everyone makes multiple calls as needed (myself included). Because of this, those 4 hours can go extremely quick. So, for those who found it important to contact their loved ones (as I did), they needed to establish their position on a phone line as soon as they could.

Whoever uses the phone first depends mainly upon which cell the CO opens first at 6pm. Once the first 4 people are on each of the 4 phones, this is when the order begins to establish. Another person will check with the current user to see if anyone has already called "next" after him, and if not, they'd call "next" after the first person using it, then another person would solidify their place in line by calling "next" after the last person, and so-on and so-forth. It's a pretty simple and easy system, and all of the guys appear easygoing and relatively respectful of one another, so there weren't any altercations over phone time. The most that would happen would be that the order on a specific phone may get confused and the guys would have to re-establish who was next on the list. Although there were never any altercations (contrary to some phone access stories I've heard take place in actual prison), it was important to make your presence known. No one was going to make sure you used the phone, so if you wanted to use it, it was your job to determine who was next, and make sure you solidified your space in a line. This serves as a microcosm for life itself. No one in life is going to give you anything, so if you want something, regardless of what it is, it is ultimately up to you to go out and put in the necessary work to attain it.

A-15, the cell I'm occupying while in A-1, was somewhat cold, bland and depressing, just as I'm sure the rest of them are. As soon as you enter the cell, the twin, steel, manila colored bunk beds are straight ahead, each containing a blue twin sized mattress. I honestly wouldn't even go as far as calling it twin size, as it seemed even smaller than this, but that's the only size equivalent there is. There is a small stainless-steel sink and lidless toilet immediately to the right, with a small mirror the size of a single sheet of 8x11 paper above the sink. There is a steel desk and stool in between the toilet and the bunk beds. To the left, there is a small single shelf with hooks underneath where books and other belongings can be stored. Behind the bunks is a small window that shows the construction occurring, as JRDC is currently undergoing expansion. I believe that they will be putting the commissioner's office right here in the jail instead of having it at the courthouse. I guess that, in some ways, this will be more convenient. Instead of having to travel to the courthouse to see the commissioner after being initially locked up, this office will now be connected to the jail. This window also gives me a view of the new inmates arriving, as it looks outward to the side of the jail where the transporting unit arrives to drop them off. The floor is a dismal gray and the walls are manila colored, brick interior.

The cell is cluttered with penciled writing, all over the walls and underneath the top bunk (I read most of what was there, as I slept on the bottom bunk.) It consisted of everything from obscenities ("fuck the law", "fuck the world", drawing of a naked woman), to positive messages ("stay positive", "get out, stay out"), to gangs ("MS-13"), different Annapolis neighborhoods ("20 Boys", "1800 Block ABC"), and odes to those from Annapolis who were taken too soon ("Long Live Drop", "Long Live Jo."). While in A-1, you're locked in your cell for a total of 19 hours per day. Because of this, often time, reading the writings on the walls is the only source of entertainment available.

One of the main differences between jail (where I am) and prison is the length of one's stay. Jail is short term, around 3 years or less, while prison sentences are longer. Therefore, it more so benefits those in jail to be reserved, calm, and receptive to the rules and policies of the institution. I have no problem with this, as this is my natural demeanor on the outside. I'm pretty calm, reserved, and generally slow to anger. I try to only concern myself with business that directly affects me. Everyone here is a relatively short stint away from returning home or being transferred to a prison if serving a longer sentence. So, there is nothing that any of them want to do in order to jeopardize their situations or add any additional time to their sentences. I knew this coming in, and it gave me a little more comfort when processing, the fact that I'll be here for the next 2 months. I was even more relieved to find that my first cellmate in A-15 shared the same sentiments as I.

Mr. Lewis, as the guards called him, or "Dread", as he was once known years ago on the street (he no longer has dreadlocks), is my first cellmate while here in A-15. He is a little shorter than me, brown skinned, heavy-set man who is around 40 years of age. He is from the Glen Burnie/Brooklyn area, the northern parts of Anne Arundel County. He attended Old Mill High School but stopped after 10th grade. He wears a black kufi during the day, which indicates to me that he is most likely Muslim. He came into the cell with a clear trash bag full of belongings: letters, personal items and materials, and a few books. Dread had already been locked up for a while in another jail and had done time prior to that as well. He was sentenced to 10 years this time around on drug charges. His hope is, with good behavior and the implementation of a new drug law, he'll be able to come home in 4-5 years if he's able to enroll into a drug program. He will only be at JRDC for the next few days, then predicts being transported to a state facility this upcoming Wednesday (I learned this is when transporting of inmates to other facilities occurs), where he will serve the remainder of his sentence. Dread was very laid back and easygoing. I think that he sensed that about me as well, along with the fact that this was my first time here, and we began to take a liking towards one another.

The orange, rubbery cups that inmates are issued are small. If you want to have any additional utensils or food (bigger cups, bowls, food, snacks, clothing, etc.) outside of what you're issued upon arrival, then you must place an order through commissary. Dread gave me a larger, clear plastic cup and bowl to have and use during my stay, 2 less things that I will need to order while here. He also taught me how to properly tie my blue sheet under my mattress to make it fitted. He is an avid chess player. He tells me stories of challenging and well experienced opponents he's beaten while doing time in other jails. We talk about politics, current events, and definitely music. He tells me stories about his heydays as a drug dealer, for which I am a more than willing and keen listener. Some of the stories that stick out to me the most involve him buying a Porsche from one of his clients in exchange for $900 worth of cocaine, a situation where he robbed someone he knew, only to have been sitting in a bullpen cell with that same person a few years later, and how over the course of his time dealing, he touched upwards of $1 million. With the rap music to which I've listened all of my life, to the classic 'hood' movies to which I know every word, I found it compelling to hear the stories of a person who lived that lifestyle firsthand, and to also see and hear about the consequences he's had to suffer for deciding to live that way.

He spoke to me about some of his experiences in prison; not jail, which made me more than thankful for only having to be in this place for such a short period of time. His tales consisted of everything from crooked CO's, to romantic sexual relationships between female CO's and male inmates, to friction with different cellmates, to problems within the Muslim community of men that he had been appointed to lead during his stay on particular tiers. However, for me, his recollections involving phone time in prison were most telling.

As stated earlier, there weren't any problems involving phone use in here thus far. On the other hand, Dread spoke about how using the phone in prison, if you were an average inmate and not gang affiliated, could be rather difficult. Essentially, each gang claimed a phone. On the particular tier (in whichever prison) where Dread stayed, he described it as the Bloods having a designated phone, BGF (Black Guerilla Family, a notorious prison gang) having a designated phone, and the Muslims (although not a street gang, they are a big community in prison) having their designated phone. No inmates not of these groups were to use the phones, and if they attempted, it would be a problem. Dread stated that the Muslims, being that they weren't a gang and because of the principles they strived to practice, would allow regular inmates time to use their phone. But overall, according to him, phone access for regular inmates was such a cause for concern that another phone had to be installed on this particular tier for them, as months were going by with them not being able to contact their loved ones.

In another instance, Dread explained how he was once housed on a tier where the phone was basically controlled by 1 inmate (he didn't specify if this was the only phone on this particular tier). This inmate happened to be a Crip gang member. Out of fear of violence from this particular inmate, no other person housed on this tier attempted to use this phone. However, Dread stated that, for reasons unbeknownst to him, this notorious inmate respected him, and allowed only him to use the phone out of all of the other inmates. "Ahk (an affectionate slang term that's used for Muslims), you can use that phone. But, once you're finished, just let the phone hang," the inmate would say to him. One man that induces such fear and reluctance into a group of men that something as simple as using the phone is seen as a dangerous action is mindboggling to me. Of course, I had to ask myself if I were in such a situation, what would I do? Honestly, I probably would've conformed, just as all of the other inmates on that tier did. This isn't to say that I'd plan to spend my entire time sentenced under the dictatorship of an inmate, a person who has no effect on when I ultimately regain my freedom. I think this is more of a case of knowing which battles to fight. If I am not being physically attacked, harmed, or being forced into any compromising positions, then not being able to use a particular phone would be something that I could probably endure. I'm confident that such situations, while unfortunate, are a harsh reality within jails/prisons across our country. There are countless stories of various inmates using fear tactics, threats, intimidation, and/or violence to gain leverage, power, and insert their dominance upon those with whom they are housed; circumstances that have thus far remained, and of which I intend to keep foreign to my life.

Judging from what I've seen since being his cellmate, Dread's faith is very important to him. He is a Muslim. I'm not sure when he began his spiritual journey, but I am aware that the Islamic religion is the fastest growing in the World, and that many African American men convert to Islam while serving time in prison. For this, I'm sure there are a host of different theories. My belief is that Islam, while a globally recognized religion for all people, has spoken directly to and resonated with the African American male in a way that other religions may have not. This, in my opinion, can be attributed greatly to the widespread popularity and following that the Nation of Islam has amassed within the African American community over the past half century.

While I consider myself Christian, I have close friends who practice Islam, and I believe that both religions adhere to many of the same principles. I have also always sought, and gained, great inspiration from the words of brilliant orators who've practiced the religion like Malcolm X and Minister Louis Farrakhan. Their messages have always resonated with me, particularly as it pertains to the African American community: doing for self, pooling together our own resources, being positive examples within our own communities, and no longer looking to outside races or institutions to "save" us, when we have all of the necessary tools within our communities to aid ourselves. Dread is teaching himself Arabic, the language spoken by many nations throughout the Islamic World. While locked in our cell from that stretch of 8:30am-6pm, I can periodically hear him, from his top bunk, reading aloud and reciting Arabic words to himself from an instructional book. He also has a miniature Quran that he reads on occasion. However, his allegiance and outward expression of his faith is most shown through his daily prayer regimen.

One of the 5 Pillars of Islam is that all those who practice are to pray 5 times per day, at very specific times throughout the day (before sunrise, midday, late afternoon, sunset, between sunset and midnight.) While praying, they are to face the Holy Islamic city of Mecca. In January of 2017 for my 30th birthday, accompanied with close family and friends, I traveled to Cairo, Egypt. Outside of seeing the Pyramids of Giza in person, one of my most memorable moments of that trip was witnessing practicing Muslims answer the calls to prayer. I remember it being a sunny Saturday afternoon in Cairo, and we were amongst the rustle and bustle of the city natives. People were out running errands, walking the streets, and enjoying time with their families, as most of us do on a nice weekend. Then, the call to prayer began blaring in the streets through speakers that were placed on the tops of various buildings, and it appeared as if most of the city stopped. I saw people immediately ready themselves for prayer, taking bows on their hands and knees and pray in unison. Up to this point, I had seen this on TV, but never in person. It was incredible to witness firsthand.

Prior to him praying, Dread would go over to our small sink, run water in his hands and proceed to rinse his face and feet, as it is a ritual, for Muslims are expected to be clean before prayer. He uses the red windbreaker jacket that we were issued to cover the toilet in our cell. If both of us are in our cell, prior to covering the toilet with the jacket, he always turns and asks me "You gotta get over here?" I'd always answer "Nah man. Do your thing." This was a polite gesture to make sure I didn't have to use the bathroom before the toilet went off limits during his time of prayer. One day, after watching him perform a prayer, I asked Dread what the significance was of him covering up the toilet. He stated that, in the Quran, it speaks about the presence of feces being prohibited while prayer is taking place, and that you are to pray in, under normal conditions, a clean environment. So, in an act of symbolism, he throws the jacket over the toilet. I later learned that the Quran states that the entire Earth is a place of prayer, except the toilet and the graveyard. His gesture now makes perfect sense. Being that he did not have an official Muslim prayer mat on which to pray, Dread would use the blue hand towel that we each were issued, lay it in front of him, and proceed to perform his 5 daily prayers on it. He would perform his gestures, bowing on his hands and knees and quietly reciting his prayers in Arabic.

One night, while all of the inmates were in the dayroom watching TV, I remember walking past our cell, briefly looking through the small window of our unit door, and witnessing Dread perform his last prayer for that day. He was on his hands and knees of the jailhouse floor, in darkness, completely submissive, reciting his prayers. During that moment, I thought how this may be one of the most beautiful things I've had a chance to see, and not just while being in jail, but period. It was more than the act of Dread praying, but rather the discipline and the dichotomy exhibited each time he does so. How can an act so beautiful be witnessed in a place so horrific? In a place that has, historically, been designed to mentally break young African American males like he and I, a place where many experience the most decrepit, depressing, and demoralizing conditions and circumstances of their lives, Dread's faith seemingly remains unaffected. And if I see the effort Dread makes, even in such conditions and void of the resources that I'm sure he possesses during his prayers on the outside, then I know Allah sees it as well, and is pleased. Each day, Dread maintains his prayer regimen, and he makes it a point to not allow being confined after it. He uses the resources around him (which are few while incarcerated), completely humbles himself, and continually adheres to the Islamic guideline of offering one's gratitude and praise to the Most High 5 times per day. Having watched this sequence take place since being Dread's cellmate, it has provided me with two constant reminders; that God is always present, even in the places that you may fear He has abandoned, and that beauty can be found in even the most grim conditions, but it is up to us to locate.

There were a couple of important things that occurred during my first few days behind bars. The first was that I made it a point to complete a form requesting to work while in jail. During the first conversation I had with my mother while on the phone in the receiving unit, she stated that the CO working at the front lobby, Mr. Somerville, gave her some important information. He informed her that once I go through receiving and get settled, that I should complete a work request form as soon as possible. When inmates who've already been sentenced receive jobs while at JRDC, a day is removed from their sentence for each day they work, or "day-for-day." This inevitably makes their release date sooner than originally scheduled. The CO then went on to tell my mother that because he could sense that I was sensible and not a troublemaker, he would call to put in a good word for me to ensure that I am able to land a job during my sentence. This information was pivotal, for if there are any opportunities available that will allow me to decrease my time, I am more than willing to explore. I also have never been a stranger to hard work. So, whichever job I'm able to land while here, I'll consider it to be the most important job I've had up to this point in my life, because my freedom will be my payment. Once I received this information, I put in my request immediately.

Secondly, on Monday March 18th, I was seen by a Case Manager, as all inmates do within their first few days of being on A-1. She was a black woman; I'd estimate to be between her late 40's and mid 50's. We spoke about the nature of my charge and conviction, and my criminal history. She also asked me questions about my employment and education history. Most importantly, she informed me of the best news that I received since being here, that my scheduled release date was for April 23rd. This date was a few weeks earlier than the date that I initially estimated, May 13th, as I was originally given a 60-day sentence. Now, I had heard about the "good behavior" concept prior to coming to jail: that original sentences get reduced pending the inmates practicing good conduct and not having any infractions (fights, contraband, violent episodes, etc.). However, I was unaware that when scheduling an inmate's release date, they already factor the "good behavior" time into the equation. That's to say that your scheduled release date already has your good time (which is an estimated 40% of your sentence) calculated, assuming you receive no infractions during your sentence. Your good time can be stripped, however, with your sentence increasing as a result, only if you do happen to violate any jail codes of conduct. So, what was originally supposed to be a 2-month prison stint, was decreased to roughly 38 days, as long as I behaved myself. That for sure wouldn't be a problem.

All of what I've written up to this point has stemmed from pure observation over my first few days of incarceration; observation of what is my new home for the month, and observation of the people with whom I've been housed. I did not specifically document anything that took place within my first few days of being here, as the idea to do so hadn't struck me until about 4 days into my sentence. The documentation of my daily activities begins March 19th, 2019.

Tuesday, March 19th, 2019

"Smith!!" I hear my last name being called from my cell at around 12:40am. A CO, accompanied by a nurse, bring me out of my unit to provide (another) urinalysis for drugs and alcohol. This is a standard procedure performed by the jail on any inmate who has put in a request to work. However, I already provided one sample the day before, so I'm not really sure why another one has been requested from me again so quickly. I hope there aren't any issues, because I know I haven't used or drank anything since being here. I provided the sample, nonetheless, then went back into my cell and went back to sleep.

Falling completely asleep in my cell is a task all unto itself. For one, the beds are too small for grown men. There's no such thing as stretching out. Also, there's nothing comfortable about attempting to sleep on a steel frame. There's no give to the mattresses on which we lay at all. Every time I try to shift to get comfortable, I can feel the screws from the steel frame piercing through the mattress and into my sides. On top of this, the lights in the cell never turn off completely. There's always a light that's kept on in each cell, preventing absolute darkness. While I do understand that this is for safety purposes, it makes it much more difficult when actually trying to get some rest. And, if all of this isn't enough, there's Dread's snoring. I'm almost certain that he could wake up the entire A-I unit if our door was kept open one night for the rest of the inmates to be exposed. I'm not exaggerating at all. I've heard some loud snorers, but this is on an entirely different level. The first night staying in the cell with him, he said to me "If I'm snoring too loud, just hit the bottom of the bunk." I didn't think it would be a concern, so I didn't pay his statement too much attention, but rather just appreciated his polite gesture. I couldn't have been more wrong. One day while we were up, both of us lying in our respective bunks, I finally broke down and mentioned his snoring.

"Man, you weren't playing when you said something about your snoring earlier." I said, laughingly.

"Yea, I was loud?" Dread replied.

"Yea man. It's pretty loud." I replied back.

We both laughed about this. From that point on, he attempted to muffle his nightly snores by putting tissue paper in his nostrils while he slept. It would work for a little while, but as the night went on, the noise would eventually creep back to its original volume. I know that there's essentially nothing that I can do in this situation, for I am in no position to alter a person's sleep pattern, and there are no sleep specialists present in JRDC to conduct testing on Dread to determine why he snores at such an elevated volume. All I can do is chalk this up as a minor inconvenience and appreciate that Dread even made an effort to stifle the sound.

I woke out of my sleep suddenly to see Dread on the floor, and he wasn't praying this time. Somehow he managed to fall from his bunk. He said that he was attempting to get in his bunk by stepping on the stool and hoisting himself, as he normally does. This time, I don't think he jumped high enough, and fell to the floor. After making sure he was ok, we both shared a laugh about this, then went back to sleep.

Breakfast generally comes between 4:30 and 5am every morning. The sounds of the CO or tier-runners (inmates whose job it is to deliver the trays to each of the tiers throughout the jail) yelling "trays" is indication that it's time to wake up to receive your meal. Our meals are served to us through the tray hatch on the cell doors in A-1. The food is placed on thick, blue plastic trays, comprised of 3-4 square compartments where each dish is placed.

This morning's meal was grits, eggs, and bread that is cut and served in a style similar to cornbread, but not as moist. It tastes more like a biscuit. I call it "cake bread." I didn't eat any of the breakfast this morning; I only drank the chocolate milk. I'm hardly ever hungry during the time breakfast is being served in here. I'm a morning person, but this is way too early for me to eat anything. On top of this, I haven't been too enticed by what's been served thus far. We all have heard the stories about jail/prison food, and so far it's been living up to its reputation. It sounds crazy, but I knew that when coming here, I would not eat as much as I do on the outside. Not saying that I plan on starving myself, but I've already mentally prepared myself for this aspect of being incarcerated. I need to drop a few pounds anyway, so I look at this as a way of quickly being able to do so.

I went out in the dayroom at 7:30am, as we're only given between then and 8:30am to be out in the morning on A-1. I watched whatever was on TV at the time and skimmed through the Capital Gazette (Anne Arundel County newspaper), but I didn't really find any of what I read interesting enough to remember. Before you know it, we were back in our cells so that the bail reviews could begin.

Lunch here is normally served between 11:30am and 12pm. Today, we had hot dogs and beans, string beans, pineapples, and chips. I only ate the pineapples and the chips.

The time we are locked in is usually spent laying down or sleeping, but Dread and I also talk some to pass the time. We speak about everything from his previous stints in jail/prison, his drug dealer tales, hardships with his former wife, his past business ventures (he once had a food truck in Baltimore that eventually went under due to family mismanagement when he went away to prison), and possible future endeavors (he has an idea of opening a mobile barber shop once he comes home).

Dinner is usually served in here between 4:30 and 5pm. I'm not even home from work at this time when on the outside. The majority of America isn't either, I'm sure. All of the meals in here are served a lot earlier than to what I'm accustomed. On today's menu, we had meat and mash potatoes with gravy, mixed veggies, and a chocolate chip cookie. I ate a portion of the main dish, all of the vegetables, as well the entire cookie. After dinner, we usually remain awake, because only an hour or so remains before we are allowed back into the dayroom.

At 6pm, the CO came around to each cell, unlocked the doors, and allowed us into the dayroom. The waiting lists for the phones began to establish, and inmates began removing chairs from where they had been previously stacked. I pulled up a chair and began watching TV, along with the rest of the inmates.

At around 7pm, for an unknown reason, the entire A-1 was placed on lockdown, and we all had to return to our cells. However, it was brief, as we were let out and back into the dayroom about 5 minutes later.

After returning to the day room again, I was able to get on the phone and speak to moms. While in here, I gave her my email password. I told her to check my email daily to see if I receive any information or updates regarding job opportunities, and/or the status of my current state of employment. She said that an e-mail came from the union representative at my current employer, DC Child and Family Services Agency (CFSA), stating that the human resources department still has yet to make a decision concerning my reinstatement, but that I could expect one to be made soon. At this point, I consider no news as being good news. As of now, CFSA is aware of my situation, and knows that I may potentially have to serve some time, but they are unaware that I've already begun my sentence. My hope is that they don't reach a decision until I am finished serving my sentence, or at least closer to completion.

After spending a few evenings with the same individuals in the dayroom, it's only natural that you begin to speak to a few of them. This may come out of shared interests, such as something being shown on the TV (game, movie, news, etc.) about which you both may voice resembling points, or if someone asks for another's assistance, such as with setting up a phone account or with how to order commissary. When this occurs, you sometimes gain insight into why another person is here. You quickly find out that everyone in jail is not actually a criminal, and, often times, their situations don't even warrant their being here.

For example, this evening, I spoke to a black guy who arrived in A-1 a few days after me. Tall, dark skinned brother, 35 years old. He's never been to the state of Maryland. He was actually apprehended during a layover at BWI airport, as he was on his way back home to San Antonio, Texas, after celebrating his birthday with his girlfriend in the Dominican Republic. While he was on vacation, out of the country, an ex-girlfriend made a false claim that he allegedly assaulted her, and a warrant was issued for his arrest. So, because of this false charge, which was made in a completely different state than where he was arrested, he had to be taken into custody, away from his family and job, and undergo the necessary proceedings in order to regain his freedom and prove his innocence.

This means that, of course, money has to be spent by inmates and their families, on bail/bail bondsman, transportation home if bail is granted, and a proper defense. All of these expenses are unexpected. Also, being that he's in Maryland, it makes it that much more difficult for his family to come visit him, and him losing his job becomes a stronger possibility with each day he spends incarcerated. At his bail review, he was offered no bail on his charge. So, as to my understanding, he must sit here until he receives another bail review with the hopes that it is granted, or until the state of Texas finally decides to have him extradited. All of this is happening prior to any conviction, but based solely upon allegation. This was only one example of hearing about a person not receiving the fairest treatment from the system while here. I'm sure that, before I leave, I'll encounter more.

We locked back in at 10pm. Dread and I had a great conversation about music and our feelings on the new age rap as well as the rap to which we grew up listening. Dread is a fan of lyricism and storytelling in rap, as am I. Nas, the God MC, is his favorite rapper, as he is also one of mine. Once he mentioned this, it was all I needed to hear. We started bonding even more, recited some of our favorite Nas lyrics to one another, and spoke about his ability to paint pictures with his words. We talked about one of his songs in detail, "One Love," from his classic Illmatic album. I was all too happy to hear that Dread had concluded the same thing about this song that I had some time ago; that Nas' third verse in this song was actually depicted in a scene in the Hype

Williams directed, cult classic film Belly. To me, the fact that one of his verses was used to create a movie scene, speaks so much to Nas' level of genius, his attention to detail, and overall ability to convey a story as a writer.

Dread and I also spoke about the new age, "mumble" rap that has become popular over the past decade. Of course, he said that he isn't a big fan of it. I understood his position. I explained to him that I'm not the hugest fan of everything that is released in that subgenre either, because similar to him, I will always be a big supporter of substance and lyrics. I do, however like some of this music for its melodies, beats, and cadences. I believe that both of the style of rap music, that which is lyricism heavy and that which doesn't focus on lyrics as much, can co-exist, as long as there is a healthy balance. Furthermore, I believe that each style, in a sense, is necessary, as it broadens the spectrum of rap music and hip-hop culture as a whole, and, as a result, allows the culture to ascend to certain platforms where it once was not present.

Dread grew up in the 90's, and he was really in the streets during this time. He was heavily involved in a life of crime and experienced both its highs and lows. These experiences were what most of the prominent rappers during this era were talking about in their rhymes. More than simply entertainment, they provided the real-life soundtrack to his life, the good and bad that came with choosing to live an illegal lifestyle. This is why I understand the certain attachment he maintains to that era of music. I explained to Dread the reason that I believe that many people are fascinated with rap music, and the stories told by the artists, is because, whether embellishing or completely truthful, these tales are so far removed from the everyday lives of ordinary people, including myself, that it becomes a form of entertainment.

On a grander scale, I further explained to Dread that, in my belief, the aforementioned is also the reason behind America's fascination with gangsters, criminals, and the underworld as a whole. America, especially minorities in America, love the underdog story. It is very seldom that those who come from the meekest of circumstances grow to prominence and acquire fame, riches, and/or wealth. So, when they do, we as Americans tend to celebrate it. These conditions (although self inflicted due to the choice of their work) seem to be amplified more in the sake of a person who sells drugs, as violence, death, and/or a lengthy jail sentence are elements that are consistently present for those who've made this lifestyle choice. So, the masses or people unaffiliated with that part of the culture, may view the decision to consistently risk one's life and freedom for a better lifestyle as stupidity. But, through the lens of the same underdogs who may not know or have been shown a better way, it is seen as a form of courage and valiance.

We both decided to go to sleep following our great conversation. We had only been bunked together since the 15th, but our convos made it seem as if we'd known each other longer than 4 days. Dread had a strong feeling that he would be getting transported to another facility tomorrow, as he would be doing his sentence in a state facility, and JRDC normally does their transporting of inmates on Wednesdays. I guess we both will see once tomorrow comes.

Yesterday, I started a calendar to mark off each day spent here once completed. Dread told me not to do it, as he feels that only makes the time go slower. This may be true for someone with a longer sentence, but I don't think so in my case. I only have a few weeks here, and I want to make sure I always know how much closer to my freedom I am. So, with that being said, consider this as another day down.

Wednesday, March 20th, 2019

Breakfast this morning was small, silver dollar pancakes, cereal, and a slice of bologna. I only ate the pancakes. They weren't IHOP, but they were good, nonetheless.

The CO came back to our cell around 5am, just after breakfast had been served. "Mr. Lewis, get your stuff together, your heading out," he instructed. It was Dread's time to be moved to a different jail, a state facility where he would be serving the remainder of his sentence. We spoke about this over the course of the time that we were cellmates. His hope was simply to be moved to a facility that is quiet and not too far for his family to travel to visit. Unfortunately, this isn't information known by the inmate prior to their relocation. This is an unknown that I'm sure the system could easily address and change, as it would, in turn, bring less stress upon the inmate as well as their families in regard to visitation.

Dread packed up his belongings and put them into his clear plastic trash bag. We dapped each other and wished one another good luck. I gave him my phone number and Instagram information and told him to give it to his lady so that we could stay in contact. Prior to him stepping into the back of the van once outside, he knocked on the outside of my cell window (the one located behind the bunks) and threw his fist up to me and smiled. I returned the same gesture. He then stepped in the back of the van (shackles on both hands and ankles) and was transported off. Dread was a cool and very solid individual overall. He's smarter than I think he may even realize. He's already proven he has a mind for business from the stories he told about his past ventures. I hope that he uses those skills to execute some of the other good business ideas he shared with me while here. Dread made a great impression on me. I pray that he remains safe in whatever prison he ends up doing his bid in. And that he encounters nothing but success in all that he does in the future.

Around 8:30am, I was called out of my cell, along with 2 other inmates, to head to the medical department. I was told that I needed to have a physical, as all inmates in the jail are required to have, but especially for inmates who intend to work. I waited for a little while with 5 other inmates in a separate room, then was finally called into the nurse's office. Once there, I was expecting to have a full-blown physical conducted, but I only had to answer a few general questions about my health history, and a stethoscope was used to check my breathing.

After this, I was asked if I wanted to have my blood drawn to test for hepatitis C, HIV, and Syphilis. This was purely optional, but I decided to do so. I figured that, while here on my short stay, it wouldn't hurt to take advantage of whatever free resources I could. I went into a different room where another nurse asked me some more questions. She then used a needle to draw blood from my right forearm. Afterwards, she stated that the results would be in within 7-10 business days, and if my tests came back negative, they would be sent to me via mail. However, if positive, then I would have to call the jail's medical facility to receive them via phone. I fully expect to be given my results via mail while I'm here.

I was back in the cell from my medical visit by 9:30am. By 10am, my new cell buddy arrived. I was wondering how long it would be before another inmate was sent to this particular cell. I even thought that, by some mistake or miracle, I could have the cell to myself for at least a few days. I should've known better though. New inmates are constantly arriving to JRDC, and A-1 is always the first place they are housed upon arrival. The thought of having an unaccompanied cell was short lived.

My new cellmate's name was Kevin. He was a short, but sturdy, white guy with black hair, 31 years of age. Once he arrived, Kevin quickly acknowledged me ("What's up?"), and I did the same with him. He then set up his bed and belongings on the top bunk, and immediately went to sleep. He looked disheveled, like he had a long night prior, so I could understand the urgency with which he wanted to get to a unit and rest.

Lunch came at its normal time. Today we had Sloppy Joe sandwiches (haven't had one of these since a youngin'), string beans and corn, mashed potatoes, and cake. I only ate the string beans and corn, a little bit of the mashed potatoes, and the cake.

After lunch, Kevin and I spoke briefly. I found out that he was from Lothian, MD, a small country town in southern Anne Arundel County that borders Upper Marlboro of Prince Georges County. It's about 10-15 minutes away from my hometown of Shady Side, MD. I had family in this town as well. Both of these neighboring small towns, along with a few others (Deale/Churchton, Edgewater, Galesville, Davidsonville, Friendship) make up what is known as the greater South County (SoCo) area. If you add the populations of all of these towns, it may roughly equate to that of Annapolis.

Kevin briefly attended Southern High School in Harwood, Md., but also attended various other high schools in Calvert County. We actually ended up knowing some of the same people. Southern was the school from which nearly all of my family and friends graduated. I also attended Southern for my 8th grade year (during this time, the middle school was too overcrowded so 8th graders attended high school), but then attended Severn School in Severna Park, Md. for the remainder of my high school years.

It turned out that Kevin did actually have a long night, which explained why he was so tired when he came in. He spent most of the night before being chased by police, and then the majority of the early morning in a holding cell in the receiving unit. Unfortunately, this wasn't Kevin's first time here. This time, he is being jailed for an escape charge. He was originally charged with multiple 1st and 2nd degree assaults, for which he had been placed on house arrest pending his upcoming court date. However, he said that following an evening of heavy drinking and a bad argument with his girlfriend, he made the stupid decision of cutting off his ankle monitor. "Yeah, that was definitely a stupid decision to do that," Kevin explained. At least he was able to admit this much. After doing that, I seriously doubted that he'll be granted bail at his hearing. In no way am I throwing stones though. I can't, because an equally stupid decision I made landed me in here right beside him.

Dinner this evening was macaroni style noodles with meat, similar to Hamburger Helper. It was served with a small side salad, fruit, and cornbread. I only ate the fruit and cornbread.

6pm came and we were finally allowed out of our units. I'd been hoping that I would be leaving A-1 soon. I had a feeling that this would be the day, as today would make my 6th evening on this tier, I had already been seen by the Case Manager, and most inmates are usually moved to an actual unit after about a week or so.

"Smith!! Get your things. You're moving out tonight," the CO on duty yelled. Hell yea, it's about damn time!! I was too so excited. I was finally leaving A-1 and being moved to an actual housing unit. No more 19-hour lockdown and 5 hours of phone access per day. I went to my cell and began packing my things. But, in the process of doing so, the CO came to my unit and stated that it was actually another Smith that was moving from A-1 tonight. "You sure?" I asked. "Yea, Ryan Smith is moving. You're Darren, right?" Damn!! My hopes of relocating quickly went away, but, it can't be much longer before I'm gone from here. I can feel it. I've had more than my fair share of A-1, and it was time for me to relocate to a unit where the amenities weren't as restricted.

I swept the inside of the cell, then went back out to the dayroom and continued watching TV with the rest of the guys. They were flipping between Jurassic Park, and the Celtics vs. 76ers basketball game. Philly ended up winning 118-115.

After a while, I decided to hop on the phone and make a few calls. I found out from moms that my close homeboy Jaysin reached out to her yesterday to see when my visiting hours were. Visiting hours/days here vary depending upon what tier a person has been placed. I definitely didn't expect anyone to come here to visit me, although I know a select few, like my mother and Ms. Elizabeth, will visit regardless of my wishes. I am only doing a little over 30 days here, an extremely short time when put in perspective. Therefore, I don't want to over-dramatize my situation with visits, as I know this is a very short stay. Also, I know all of my friends have hectic schedules with work and their own families. Furthermore, I mentally prepared myself for this short isolation from my family and friends to act as an additional punishment. In a weird way,

I almost don't want to be visited, like I am inviting this extra burden. Although I know this is hardly the case, I somewhat view visits from my loved ones as receiving a reward for my faulty decision, and I don't want that feeling. In a way, it's like I feel undeserving of their visits.

I remember famous southern rapper and activist David Banner tweeting about how he sometimes likes to "sit in a mistake for while" so that he can learn all of its aspects, with the plan being to never revisit the same error. That statement always resonated with me. I feel that not having any visitors would allow me to sit more in my own mistake. However, I could never shun away any visits from friends and family who are aware of my situation. I have an incredible support system, so I'd be more than grateful and appreciative if any of them made the time to visit. I just will not hold it as an expectation.

I noticed a few new faces here in A-1 this evening. Although I didn't know any of them, I could tell from how they talked, and what they talked about, that a few of them were mid 20-year olds from Annapolis. They also appeared to know one another. Being that Annapolis is such a small city, with a smaller black population, this is not at all uncommon. Most black people in the Annapolis area are either related, went to school with one another, or know mutual people. They all also hang in the same places and attend the same events, so if you wanted to get in contact with a specific person, they wouldn't be hard to locate. They say 6 degrees of separation implies that all people are only 6, or fewer, social connections away from one another. I estimate it being only 1 degree of separation if you're black and from Annapolis, especially if you're in the same age bracket.

While on the phone, one of these new guys received word that his child's mother and her friends, which are also his sisters and female cousins, jumped his new girlfriend. As one can imagine, he wasn't happy about this news at all. And, judging by his reaction once off of the phone, the way in which he talked about addressing the situation once on the outside would probably land him right back in here. I hope that won't be the case.

Another one of these new Annapolis faces was one that, although I didn't know personally, I definitely recognized through being close with mutual people, and having many mutual social media friends and followers. Above all of this, I've grown familiar with his case over the past year through both mutual friends and media outlets. He and his affiliates (some of whom I also knew of through mutual friends) have been involved in, arguably, the biggest drug indictment in Annapolis in recent years for their alleged involvement in large narcotics distribution throughout the area. Their stories, and pictures of their faces, have been in The Capital consistently since last summer. As for Anne Arundel County, one could definitely consider this as a very high-profile drug case.

You miss the small amenities while in here, things that are usually at your disposal while going through your daily routine but, at times while here, you'll have to go without. For example, I keep chap stick with me at all times on the outside. Even to the point that, if I leave my crib without some, I'll make a quick stop at a gas station to replenish before I continue with my day. But, while in here, it has to be ordered with commissary, which only comes once per week. For the first few days of me being here, my lips were dry as shit, almost to the point of blistering since I've been licking them more often for moisture. I can't wait until Saturday when commissary arrives so that I can finally have some lip balm, because blistering lips is definitely an unpleasant feeling.

We locked back in our cells at 10pm. Hopefully, I'll get word about getting a job, or at least about moving from A-1 soon. Another day down.

Thursday, March 21st, 2019

Breakfast this morning was a biscuit (or something like it) with sausage gravy and oatmeal. I didn't eat any of what was served, just drank the chocolate milk that came with the meal.

There was a loud commotion that occurred this morning in cell A-13. I couldn't make out exactly what happened, but later I was told that the inmate fell out, and possibly had a seizure. The nurses and paramedics came and removed him from the cell for further treatment. I hope that he's ok.

I spoke to moms and Ms. Elizabeth this morning on the phone during the hour that we're allowed in the dayroom. Ms. Elizabeth confirmed that she was coming to visit me later this evening. I couldn't wait to see her. I know I said that I initially didn't want visitors, as I felt like I was undeserving of their time and support for me during this situation, but, I'm no fool. Anyone who would take the time to visit me while I'm here, I'm going to be beyond grateful.

Prior to going back into our cells before the start of bail reviews, I noticed the guy who arrived yesterday with the high-profile drug case talking on the phone and holding The Capital. My goal was to take the paper back into the cell with me, so that I could have something to read while locked in for the remainder of the morning/afternoon. Once he was off the phone, I asked him was he finished with it. He said that he was and gave it to me. I thanked him, and then went back into my cell.

As soon as I started looking at the paper, I saw a story involving the man who had just handed it to me, and his affiliates, on the bottom of the front page.

"Annapolis Gang Leader Sentenced to 20 Years in Prison" read the bold imprinted headline. The article highlighted intricate moments in the police's investigation, as well as each member's role within the organization, their charges, pleas entered, and sentences. Yesterday was the actual day that the alleged leader of this gang (of whom I'm also familiar through various mutual friends) received his 20-year sentence. The man who was in here with me received a sentence of 12 years for his involvement. Being that he will be doing his time in prison, I'm sure that he will only be in this unit for a few more days before being transferred to another facility. The irony that the person who handed me today's paper is the topic of one of its biggest stories is crazy to me. I'm sure I'll hear more about this case, and those involved, as time continues.

Another story I read on the front page involved the remains of a man found in a burnt car in Glen Burnie. A man named Jack Butler Nichols was charged with homicide and arson for his alleged involvement in this crime, and he is also being held here at JRDC without bail.

Anne Arundel County is one of the largest counties in the state (in terms of population), yet it is still roughly half the population size of Prince Georges and Montgomery counties. Anne Arundel is also nowhere near as urbanized as these two counties, or Baltimore (city and county). Because there are less people inhabiting concentrated areas in Anne Arundel than there are in the other aforementioned areas, I believe that there are less documented cases of violent crime as a result. So, whenever I hear about murders/homicides in this county, like the one I just read about, I do tend to take notice, for these things don't happen as often here as with the other more populous counties in the state.

After reading the stories in the paper that interested me the most, I attempted to do the crossword puzzle that was on the back page. I definitely didn't think it would be that difficult. I only managed to get a few words (I believe). I spent way more time deciphering the clues than actually filling in words. It was a brain exercise that, above all else, helped to pass the time while locked in, so it served its purpose.

Lunch today was tacos, beans, cabbage, and a gingerbread cookie. I only ate the cabbage and the cookie.

It was rainy and gloomy for most of today. I looked out of the window that faced the inmate drop-off area and watched the nasty weather for a little. I read more of the paper, then laid back down.

This evening's dinner wasn't too bad at all. It was a turkey and rice dish with cake for dessert. I ate everything today, except for the 2 slices of white bread that usually comes with each lunch and dinner meal.

6pm came and we were let into the dayroom for the evening. The same routine ensued; phone and TV.

The CO called my name around 6:30pm saying I had a visit. I went to the visiting area and Ms. Elizabeth was waiting on the opposite side of glass. We spoke earlier that day confirming her visit, so I wasn't surprised, but it was still great to see her. We've grown extremely close over the past year, and other than my mother, she's been my hugest supporter throughout this entire ordeal, especially during the days leading up to having to turn myself in. Her, along with my mother, both set up phone accounts prior to me coming in so that I could always call and speak to them. They both also placed funds into my commissary to hold me over until my own money had been cleared.

Above all else, jail is a business, and everything in this place costs. From each second you speak on the phone to your loved ones, to the clothing you order outside of what you've been issued, to the additional food you may get through commissary, it all comes with a price. Usually it is the inmate's family and supporters who are footing the bill for these purchases, as inmates gain little to no income. Jail is an entire industry where billions are made annually at the expense of other's mistakes and misfortunes, without the same amount spent on the "rehabilitation" component. Big business it is indeed.

Since I've been in, Ms. Elizabeth and I have spoken every day, mainly about how our days have been, the latest news in black social media, and bouncing ideas off of one another. Our conversation during this visit was no different, as I shared with her my plan on making the best out of my current situation. I told her that, since I've been in, I've essentially kept record of everything I've done, from what I've eaten, stories I've read in the paper, meaningful conversations I've had, any crazy stories heard from other inmates or unordinary occurrences underwent. I told her that I would do this for the duration of my sentence, and once I'm out, compile the writings and release a memoir about my experience. She thought that this was a great idea, and that was all the motivation I needed to continue. Her support means everything to me.

After my visit, I went back to A-1 and showered. I only had one change of greens, and the briefs that I wore in here initially. Because of the lack of change of clothing, I'm only going to shower every few days, and not on a regular basis like I would if I were home. I'll only be in here for a few more weeks, so I can manage. I did order 2 pairs of boxers when I placed my commissary order, all of which should arrive on Saturday. Speaking of commissary, the $71 with which I came in and instructed the staff to be placed towards my commissary is finally showing up in my account. The CO explained to me that when cash is placed on an inmate's commissary account, it takes a few days to show, similar to how it takes a check a few days to clear. That bread should last me until the end of my sentence.

I relaxed in the dayroom for the rest of the evening until lock-in at 10pm. We watched the first round of some of the March Madness games. Villanova beat St. Mary's 61-57. Another day down.

Friday, March 22nd, 2019

Breakfast this morning was pancakes, cereal, and a slice of bologna. I only ate the pancakes.

I was able to get today's Capital again this morning prior to locking in for the remainder of the day. I read that the funeral for former MD Governor Harry Hughes was held yesterday in Annapolis. He lived to age 92 and, according to the paper, he'll be remembered most for the works he did for others.

I attempted the crossword puzzle again in today's paper, and it was just as difficult as yesterday. It helped to pass the time, so again it served its purpose.

While in the cell during the morning, I was called out of my cell so that I could meet with Ms. Kellie. This was the meeting that I had been waiting for from the moment I submitted my work requests when I arrived. Ms. Kellie is the woman who does all of the hiring in JRDC and informs each inmate of his or her new employment position. To say that I was excited was an understatement.

Ms. Kellie informed me that I had been hired for a job with cleaning and waste management; basically, a custodian. I will be working in the main lobby of the jail, and my hours will be in the early morning, from 1am to about 4am. Jail policy states that an inmate must work at least 5 hours in order to be credited for having worked that day. Ms. Kellie stated that my position is the shortest shift to work out of all the possible jobs in the jail, and I would still receive credit for working an entire day. She showed me a short orientation video for my position, and I signed some paperwork confirming me as a new hire. She stated that I would be starting tomorrow morning, and on top of it all, I'd finally be moving from A-1 and into an actual housing unit tonight! This means 24-hour access to the TV and phone, and no longer being locked in a cell for 19 hours per day.

Since I already had such a short sentence, Ms. Kellie stated that she would need to check with the records department, and my diminution sheet, to see if whether or not working while here would be to my benefit. I may not even be able to get any additional time cut from my sentence if I work and having a job would only work in my favor if an even closer release date were the result. This date has already been pushed up to April 23rd, a few weeks ahead of the originally scheduled, contingent upon the "good time" I receive. But, for each day you are credited for working, another day is removed from your sentence, also known as receiving "day-for-day." However, by law, an inmate is not allowed to receive both good time and day-for-day time. This would be cutting it close, so much so that working may not even be in my best interest.

After calculating, Ms. Kellie was able to determine that if I worked everyday beginning tomorrow, my release date would move up by an entire 10 days, making the new date April 13th! It's safe to say that working would definitely be to my benefit. I was extremely happy returning to my cell. This is the best news I've received since being here by far, and I'm more than ready to get started.

Today's lunch was a bologna and cheese sandwich on white bread with mustard on the side, a small side salad, chips, and a snickerdoodle cookie. I only ate the chips and the cookie today. I was an extremely picky eater when I was young. I used to eat a bologna and cheese sandwich for lunch at school (minus the mustard) everyday until the 5th grade. I haven't had it since. A lot of the shit that's being served in here just doesn't look that appetizing to me, so I've just been picking through meals up to this point.

Kevin was given some bad news while locked in this afternoon. He was given some documents saying that he lost 10 days of "good time" for the dirty urine sample that he gave on Wednesday, the day of his arrival. Being that he had been on house arrest, his urine is supposed to be clean. He also lost additional "good time" because of his escape charge. Being on house arrest is, in principle, the same as being detained, except for being in the comforts of your home. Therefore, all of the same rules and regulations of being in jail still apply while on house arrest. I doubt that Kevin thought about this when he decided to escape, or he did but just wasn't in the right frame of mind to care about the repercussions of his actions. Either way, he's going to pay some sort of additional consequence.

Dinner this evening was a baked chicken leg and thigh with mashed potatoes and gravy, green beans, cornbread and cake. Although the chicken was red on the inside, I ate most of it. I also ate all of the green beans and mashed potatoes.

6pm came, and we were allowed back in the dayroom. This would be my last evening of rec-time spent on the A-1 tier. The normal routine commenced; phone, inmates going back and forth to the coolers for water and ice, some groups talking amongst themselves, all the while the TV is being turned between various channels.

The first round of the March Madness games were still being played. Oregon knocked off Wisconsin, making this the first 12th seed victory over a 5th seed of the tournament. College basketball analysts always said to pay close attention to the 12th seed vs. 5th seed matchups, as there is usually a 5th seed that makes an early exit from the tournament.

Prior to lock-in for the night, the CO came out into the dayroom and informed me that I should begin gathering my things. "Smith! Go ahead and pack your stuff. You're moving. Make sure you bring your mattress too." I couldn't wait to hear these words. "Bet!" I replied. I went into A-15, threw all of my belongings issued to me in my netted laundry bag, removed my mattress from out of my bunk, and was led out of A-1 down the hall to the C-1 tier. I wasn't too sure what to expect with my new living arrangement, but I knew that anything was better than being locked in a cell for 19 of 24 hours without access to anything to keep your mind occupied.

C-1

The set up in a regular housing unit is different than how A1 was structured. While in A-1, you share a cell with one other person. But, in an actual unit, you're housed in a dormitory style set-up with about 16-20 other individuals. C-1 is a long rectangular room that used both cell-bars and walls to keep inmates contained. There are 2 rows of bunk beds on each side of the room, with 5 bunks in each row. There are two toilets and a shower, each of which had barriers separating them. The bathroom area was enclosed by a white brick-style half wall. Upon arrival, I was told by 1 of the inmates that the outside toilet was for "piss," while the toilet between the outside toilet and the shower was for "shit."

Since the dividers don't extend all the way to the ceiling, and there aren't any doors to provide full privacy, there had to be some creativity and improvisation used for whenever a person needs to perform a #2. For the defecation toilet, the inmates took extra blue bed sheets and, with the sticky label wrapper paper that's placed on deodorant bottles, taped the sheets on either side of the middle toilet as high up on the back wall as they could. They then cut holes in the opposite corners of each of the sheets. There's a large plastic bottle of soap that sits on the middle of the white brick wall. The holes of the sheets are placed over the bottle of soap, creating a small, triangular, hut-like enclosed space that allows the individual to now have some privacy while he's handling his business.

There are 3 tables that are lined up sideways, 1 in front of the other, in front of the first column of bunks on the left (if viewing the cell from the front of the room.) One of the tables had various games stacked alongside it, including playing cards, Domino's, Chess, Checkers, Scrabble, and Monopoly. There is one other table placed in front of the first column of bunks on the opposite side. There are 2 phones also located on this same side above the table, on the wall beside the bathroom area. The TV is hung in the front of the unit, in front of a thick glass screen that allows us to see people walking by in the hallway.

Moving to a housing unit does, in my opinion, have its disadvantages. Although there is 24-hour access to the phones, TV, and games, a regular housing unit does not have the open space of a dayroom, as in A-1. There is also only one shower on a housing unit that must be shared with 15-20 other individuals, while there were 3-4 showers in A-1. Since a space is now being shared with plenty of other inmates, there is also more opportunity for arguments, incidents, and potential altercations. I'm not too worried about this aspect, but I'd be a fool to not acknowledge that this element is now more present.

I took the top bed of the first bunk on the left side of the unit. All of the bottom beds had already been taken, as expected. While setting up my bed and putting my things away, one of the other inmates asked from which unit I had been moved. I told him that I had just came from A-1. "Damn, Yo just got here and already got a job!" "Hell yeah," I replied. C-1 is a working tier, so everyone who stays in this unit already has a job. Everyone in C-1 works in the kitchen, except for myself and another inmate of my same position with whom I will be working in the lobby area. It generally takes close to a month for someone to be placed at a job while here. But, due to a bit of persistence and a CO's good word, I was placed after only 8 days. This is why my answer was initially surprising, because he knew jobs weren't usually assigned this quickly. Thankfully, I was able to maneuver around that general norm and speed up the hiring process.

It was already late into the evening once I was moved to C-1, and work began shortly at 1am. I was told by another inmate, with whom I'll now be working, that a CO would come around and retrieve us once it was time to go out. I laid on my bed for the next few hours until we were called. I was a bit anxious because I wasn't fully sure of what to expect, but I was excited to get to work, nonetheless. I knew the implications that this would have on the length of my stay here. I caught the second half of the Duke vs. North Dakota State game. Duke got the W, as was expected with facing a 16 seed, and Zion Williamson put on a show in the second half. 1 more day down.

Saturday, March 23rd, 2019

1am came, and it was officially time to start my first day of work. The CO came around to make sure myself and the other inmate with whom I would be working were both up. We waited as the tier door slid open, the CO patted us down, and we each walked towards the lobby area.

Tran was the name of my co-worker. He was a short man of either Chinese or Japanese descent and 52 years of age. I found out that he was there for a DUI also and is scheduled for release on April 9th. For the past couple of weeks, he had been performing the lobby cleaning duties himself. The lobby isn't a big area at all, so normally just 1 person performs this job. However, I believe that as a result of the good word put in on my behalf, I was also assigned to this job as a favor.

Our cleaning duties consisted of:

- Sweeping and mopping the floors of the lobby, the bathrooms (3 located in the lobby), and the visiting rooms
- Washing all of the windows in the front entrance, the visiting rooms, and all of the doors that contained them
- Emptying all of the trash cans
- Placing disinfectant balls in each bathroom toilet
- Cleaning the bathroom toilets, sinks, and mirrors
- Restocking the bathrooms with napkins and toilet paper if needed

Tran showed me the order in which he has been knocking out the cleaning duties thus far. Then, I was given the task of washing all of the windows, while Tran swept and mopped the lobby and bathroom floors. Tran performs one task for each room at a time.

Tran is funny and he works well, but he needs to work on the way he delegates tasks and gives instructions. I don't have any problem with taking direction, especially when I'm new to a job or any other situation where I'm responsible for a task, but there's a certain way that adults, 2 grown men at that, should speak to one another. I understand that Tran has been the only person performing these duties for the past few weeks, but as the saying goes, "There's more than 1 way to skin a cat." I feel that because Tran has grown so accustomed to the order in which he has cleaned the lobby, he believes that his way is the only way it can and should be done. However, we weren't commissioned by the warden of JRDC to build a rocket or perform neurosurgery. We are merely washing windows, emptying trash, and mopping floors; menial tasks that lack complexity, have no particular order in how they should be completed, and don't involve much thought. We are also performing these tasks in the middle of the night without a designated supervisor instructing us on a specific way each task should be done. And, contrary to his belief, Tran is my co-worker, not my supervisor, and as long as both of us are sharing the workload, it shouldn't matter who completes certain tasks and the order in which they are finished (except for mopping, which should understandably be the last task done in each area/room cleaned). I'm interested to see how this work relationship between Tran and I will unfold in the days to come.

One of my homeboys, JaNathan Crutchfield, is a CO here and was working in the control unit in the lobby during my first morning on the job. I knew him through my cousin, as they both went to Broadneck High School together. We weren't super close, so we've mainly kept up with one another through social media. JaNathan is a big guy, about the size of an NFL offensive lineman. But, he's pretty easygoing, and an overall good guy judging from my previous encounters with him years ago. We spoke briefly. I'm sure that this isn't the first time he's seen a person in here that he knows on the outside, so I wasn't too embarrassed by this. "Just do what you got to do, and get on out of here," he said to me. Simple advice, but I'll definitely continue to apply it.

The official work title for my position was M.I.O. It stands for Minimum Inmate Outside. Only inmates with a minimum-security rating were able to work this position, because being that we were working in the lobby area, we were technically working outside of the jail. Another part of our job includes occasionally pulling trash from the visitors' parking lot across the street and emptying trash into the big compactor in the delivery section of the jail, which is also outside. It's considered a trustee position, so the jail wants to make sure that the individuals working this position will not attempt to escape if presented the opportunity. Although CO's would accompany us while performing both of these tasks, we were still given access to a part of the jail that other inmates were not. With that said, at the conclusion of each shift worked by an MIO, whether or not we go outside during that shift, we must be sent back to receiving in order to be strip-searched.

In my opinion, waiting to go back into receiving to be searched is a process that takes way longer than necessary. After Tran and I were finished working, we had to wait an additional 15-20 minutes for the receiving unit to allow us to come back. Once there, we each had to go into separate shower rooms, accompanied by a CO, and get strip-searched. Although I will now be strip searched every day, a plus to this is that I will be issued a new clean uniform to wear after each search conducted. An orange jump suit was given to me following my search, as this would now be the color of the jump suit I'm required to wear as being employed as a MIO.

When Tran and I arrived back to C-1 after our shift, the unit was empty. All of the other inmates were already at work, as their shift in the kitchen is from 2am to 9am. I definitely will not complain about having an empty unit for the entire morning once I return from work. This circumstance allots me the simple pleasure of taking a shower without being in a room full of individuals, something for which I am very grateful. And, although I don't anticipate having any issues or altercations with anyone in this unit, being alone in C-1, if only for the first part of the morning, essentially eliminates any issues that could potentially arise with another inmate, as there's literally no one present with whom I could have a disagreement. This level of assurance, although just for a few hours, is the most that I'll probably receive during my stay here.

Breakfast was served about an hour after our arrival back to the unit from work. Today's meal was grits, pineapples, potatoes (I think), and chocolate milk. I only had the pineapples. After breakfast, it was time to get some rest.

Once I woke back up later that morning, the CO informed me that I had a visitor. I knew it was my moms. She told me earlier this week that she would be here Saturday morning to see me.

This was my mother's first visit since dropping me off last Friday, and although I was a little embarrassed for her to see me in this state, I was still excited. My mother has been there for me throughout every peak and valley of my life; from my most prized accomplishments to my most embarrassing missteps. So I knew this time would be no different and that she would be in my corner, even if it means speaking through a glass. However, I'd be lying if I said that I could expect for her to see me in this manner during any point of my life, and I'm sure she shared this same sentiment. This is why I've always tried to honor my mother and treat her with respect, because I know that if all else fails, I will always have her support, especially during trying times such as now when I am unable to do for myself.

Mom's visit went well. We had a great conversation about life and the current position that I find myself. She shared with me a recent conversation that she had with my Aunt Nisey, whom I view as a second mother. She told me that, in the parking lot of the newly built Royal Farms convenient store in Shady Side, she was brought to tears as she explained to my aunt the feeling that she has of me thinking that I may be "privileged." She said that she thinks that I feel that because I come from a good background, have a great education, and have a lot going for myself that I am better than others, and that I am essentially immune from certain situations because of what I've accomplished thus far in my life. Her tears when explaining this to my aunt came from her feeling of disbelief that she raised a person that possessed the mindset of actually believing that he is "above someone." My aunt disagreed with her, stating that she doesn't see me as having this mentality, and that I don't carry myself in such a manner. Moms stated that she was reluctant to tell me this because she felt that I would be offended. I wasn't at all, as I understood her thought process.

In response, I explained to her that, on one hand, I do feel privileged, but not in the way that she has described. I do feel that, through some of the knowledge I've acquired and feats I've accomplished, I've been allotted certain opportunities and access that may not have been presented to some of my peers. However, as for allowing certain opportunities and access to make me believe that I am better than another human being, I wholeheartedly disagree. I pride myself on being a well-rounded individual, and because of this, I have friends and acquaintances across all walks of life and from numerous different circles. For each of these people I have great respect and admiration, whether or not we've reached the same heights, for we relate to one another on some level, and they all possess a certain quality or trait that I wish I had more of in myself.

One of the main things I remember about my upbringing was my mother never allowing me to bask too deeply in my accomplishments. She was always proud and congratulatory of any achievement I attained, but there were never any extra incentives involved for doing well, as this was the expectation. This instilled humility. Also, she never allowed me to sulk too deeply in my mistakes. But rather, just do what is necessary to correct them and continue moving forward, as mistakes are not definitive representations of who I am. These lessons learned as a youth are how I approach life on a daily basis as an adult. I try to remain humble and levelheaded at all times, because nothing is as good, or as bad, as it may appear, and because one's entire life can completely change for the positive, or negative, in an instant. I reminded my mother of this during our conversation, along with the fact that any mistakes I've made throughout my life, I've always admitted fault to them and have readily accepted any consequences that followed. I hope this reassured her that I am not the person that puts himself on a pedestal above others.

We also spoke about my ability to take criticism and listening to others when they make attempts to advise me. She told me that after my first DUI charge in 2011, she knew that, unfortunately, it wouldn't be my last, because my punishment wasn't harsh enough for me to have learned a lesson. Although I wanted to disagree, because I felt that this wasn't the case, how could I? Shit look where I'm at...in jail for the same thing years later. My current position wouldn't allow me to disagree with her.

I explained to my mother that I've never had any problem seeking advice or accepting criticism from others. I feel that, compared to my peers, I'm more receptive to both. However, my issue has always been being expected to take criticism in silence from those whom I know operate in the same fashion, or perform the same erroneous acts as I, if not worse. I've always found it difficult to subscribe to the "Do as I say, not as I do" mantra, particularly in adulthood. Additionally, I've come to realize that people enjoy telling others how and what they need to do to revise their wrongdoings, even when they aren't completely aware of the entire situation, as it gives them a sense of authority over that individual. To me, it's a way of placing themselves on a pedestal.

I've noticed that when a person is in trouble, especially when law enforcement has become involved, he or she has essentially stripped themselves of their ability to speak in their own defense, to provide context to the situation, or to contribute to the shaping of the narrative. That individual is now only seen through the lens of a wrongdoer, and they are now treated and spoken to as such. Anything that individual says in reference to their mistake falls on deaf ears, or is automatically written off as that person being defensive, or as an attempt to justify their mistake; an awkward space to be in altogether.

Another reason why it's so difficult to maneuver through this space is because

I know that ultimately, whatever criticism presented or advice given from my family members or supporters is coming from a place of love and care, as none of them want to see me in this state. At the same time, a part of me maintains a level of resentment towards those who feel compelled to offer their criticism while I'm already in such a defenseless position, especially when those close to me know that no one is more disappointed about my current state than myself. But ultimately, I wouldn't have to worry about harboring any animosity if I didn't allow myself to be put in this position. Regardless of how I slice it, it's still my fault.

It's Saturday, and Saturdays are for commissary. It's the only delivery day for commissary, and if you want your order by Saturday, it must be placed in the system by Wednesday of that week. Commissary is announced by 2 to 3 workers coming around to each unit with rolling bins containing clear plastic bags full of inmate's orders. They call your last name, and you come to the steel bars through which they pass your belongings. They pass you them one at a time to make sure that the correct number of each item you ordered is received. Once this is confirmed, you place whatever you ordered in either your netted laundry bag or blue bin and sign off on the order form stating that you have received your items.

Initially, I was afraid that my order wasn't received because I didn't hear my name called before the workers left, and all of the other orders had already been dispersed to the others in my unit. However, the workers came back about 20-30 minutes later to bring me my order. Since I just moved into this unit last night, the workers weren't aware of this. I'm assuming that they went to deliver orders to A-1, where I was prior, and once there, were informed that I was now in C-1.

My first commissary order consisted of some toiletries: 3-in-1 shower gel, deodorant, toothpaste, a couple pairs of boxers, a couple bags of miniature cookies, a box of crackers (similar to Ritz), a few bags of chips, a few bags of trail mix (which quickly became my favorite snack item on the commissary list) and a couple of beef & cheese sticks. Now I finally had something to snack on during the day while waiting for that delicious JRDC cuisine to be served. And if I didn't want to eat what we had on a particular day, a bag of trail mix could now serve as an alternative.

As I was lying back down, my name was called again, to my surprise. A CO came around and announced the names of those who had mail, and I happened to be one of those recipients. The last thing I expected was for my name to be called for mail, as I was only going to be in here a month. I'm not complaining though, for anything I receive from anyone on the outside indicates that I, and my current situation, was in someone's thoughts, and for that I'm extremely appreciative.

During my last visit with Ms. Elizabeth, I told her about my idea of documenting this entire crazy ass experience, and then releasing a memoir once I got out. She thought that it was great idea, so much so that she decided to show her support by providing me with the tools to get started. She ordered me a composition book and a few pens to write with. Up until then, I only had the few pieces of paper given to me upon arrival, and the mini pencils that I had been using to write grew dull very quickly. I was definitely excited about these gifts, as I won't have to scrounge around for more paper and writing utensils to continue documenting my experience. She also bought me a small handheld radio with headphones. I listen to music constantly on the outside, so not having any while in here was difficult. I hardly listen to the radio when on the outside (Bluetooth and Apple Music fazed that out for me), but 92.3, 93.9, and 95.5 will come in handy now more than ever while here. Although this was definitely a pleasant surprise, coming from her, it's not at all unexpected. That's just the type of person she is, very attentive, and genuinely enjoys giving. You may casually mention something to her, not even expecting her to remember; then, next thing you know, that same item is in your mailbox. This means a lot to me; it shows me that she is just as invested into my idea as I am. That kind of motivation is priceless.

I laid down through lunch. I'm not even sure what was served.

Most of the day consisted of lying down and/or watching whatever was on TV. Others in the unit were doing the same, along with playing some of the games that were available. Today, for the first time ever, I witnessed a table full of all white guys playing a game of spades. It was somewhat funny to see, but cool at the same time.
I know how to play, but I'm not confident enough to play with those who take the game too seriously, like many of my friends. I rather sit back and be entertained by the arguments that ensue when a person reneges, or when books aren't properly bid prior to a hand being played.

Dinner this evening was a chopped turkey, rice and gravy dish. It was served like a stir-fry. We also had string beans, bread, and cake. I ate pretty much all of the meal. So far, I'd say that this has been my favorite meal that the jail has prepared.

Later in that evening, a CO came past and told us that they would be having movie night, and to inform her if we wanted to go. At first, I wasn't going to attend. But, I figured that it would give me something to do and I heard that they serve pizza at movie night, which was enough incentive for me.

Movie night was in a classroom style room right down the hall from the unit. There were inmates from C-2 and C-3 who also came to watch. I'd say it was about 20 of us altogether. They showed Along Came Polly, with Ben Stiller and Jennifer Aniston. We watched it on a DVD player and a regular television that sat on a rolling stand, like how I remember watching movies in middle school. I wondered what determined the types of movies that would be played during these scheduled nights, because this film seemed like a completely random choice. On top of that, this movie came out like 15 years ago. It comes on channels like FX and TNT regularly. Could they not have found something more recent to play? Moreover, what made them think that a quirky romantic comedy was the movie that was most desired by a room full of grown men? But, I'm nothing but another inmate at this point, so my opinion is irrelevant.

For some reason, when I heard pizza was served at movie nights, I honestly thought that it would be ordered from an actual pizza place like Domino's or Pizza Hut. I was trippin' altogether for thinking that shit. While watching the movie, the blue trays on which we eat our meals were rolled into the room. Each tray consisted of a circular microwavable mini-pizza, chips, a snickerdoodle cookie and green juice in a plastic pouch. It may not have been Pizza Hut, but I ate my pizza like it was that evening, and without complaint. I used to eat these type of pizzas a lot growing up, and they tasted better than what we ate in here on a regular basis, so I was content with it.

I realized after watching that I actually forgot how funny Along Came Polly was. The basketball scene was my favorite, when Ben Stiller's best friend in the movie displayed great hustle, but absolutely no skill, not a speck of athletic ability, and a jump shot that was worse than Shaq at the free-throw line. His adlibs whenever he put up a jumper were classic. "Rain-Man!!" "Let it rain!!" His shot attempts were dreadful. Either they'd hit nothing but the backboard, or they didn't connect with any part of the goal at all. Another huge laugh came when Ben Stiller had to guard the overly hairy, sweaty man from the opposing team. When this same man jumped to make a play, and his chest hair and sweat connected with an entire side of Ben's face, this was, to me, one of the funniest parts in the movie. It was even shown in slow motion for dramatic effect. Filthy, yet too funny to turn away.

After the movie ended, we all went back to our respective units. I laid in my bed and relaxed for the rest of the evening. I hardly received any reception in my new radio, but I'll continue to try with the oncoming days. Another 1 in the books.

Sunday, March 24th, 2019

Work this morning was trying to say the least. Tran acted worse than a small child this morning, and it took everything in me to not fall victim to his childish behavior and give him a reaction, or to put my hands on him.

Tran has been the only person cleaning the lobby for the last couple of weeks. Because of this, I believe that he has developed an order in which he cleans, as most of us would if we were the sole person performing these tasks. But, when another person is added, the work dynamic has now slightly changed. It's 2 workers here now, so we should naturally be able to knock out our cleaning duties in less time. Neither of us is the other's supervisor, so the way we address one another should be reflective of this. Lastly, although you established an order for yourself to follow, there is no official correct order to clean the rooms that make up this area.

Tran's strategy was completing the same task in each of the rooms first before moving to another task. For example, if sweeping, he would sweep in each of the bathrooms, then the visiting rooms, and then the main lobby area. Then he would move on to trash, and would go around emptying the trash in each room. Next, he'd wash the mirrors in each of the bathrooms, and so on until he was complete. There's absolutely nothing wrong with this strategy, as this was the cleaning routine that he developed and with which he grew comfortable.

My strategy was different, and in my opinion, a little more efficient. Instead of going room to room completing one task, I would just knock out everything that needed to be done in an entire room before moving to the next, that way

I wouldn't have to come back to that room again. For example, I'd start in one of the 3 bathrooms in the lobby, and do all that was needed for that room; sweeping, scrubbing the toilets and the sink, washing the mirrors, restocking toilet paper, emptying the trash, mopping. Now that this room was completely finished, I would move to the next, and continue on until each section was complete. Lastly, I'd mop the entire main lobby area. Tran's reaction to seeing me clean the lobby in an order that wasn't as he instructed was completely immature, particularly for a grown man. Only children carry on in such a fashion when things aren't going as they wished.

I began thinking that the need to feel obeyed was some type of Asian cultural norm, or custom, for Tran. I am uncertain of this, but judging from Tran's behavior, I have a feeling that his culture places extreme importance on parental hierarchy, and the youth within an Asian household are placed under strict rules and regulations to which they are expected to adhere without the slightest challenge or sense of questioning. Being that I was younger than Tran, he may have felt he had license to talk to me as if I was one of his offspring, with an expectation to obey him in the same explicit manner as would his children. This was the only way I could justify his behavior at work this morning.

Tran cursed me out, called me stupid, and even refused to speak to me for the remainder of our shift because I didn't clean the lobby in the order in which he usually does and instructed me to do. I would ask him questions pertaining to work, such as if he had already performed a particular task (so as to not duplicate work), and he would give me the silent treatment. He went so far as to saying that he was going to report me to Ms. Kellie, the woman who hired us both, because I wasn't performing the duties in the order in which he instructed. I attempted to be the bigger person and apologized to Tran, stating that I wasn't aware that the order in which I cleaned offended him this much, but he still refused to speak to me. In no way did any of this hurt my feelings. I still continued to clean in the order that I wanted despite him and his clown ass temper tantrum.

There are many things wrong in this scenario, but I'll try to highlight just a few. First, the fact that you expect an adult to follow your orders when you haven't been assigned as a supervisor or a person of authority is troubling. We're both inmates in a correctional facility, so neither of us is in a position to dictate to the other. I'm always in agreement with making reasonable requests or suggestions. But, I will not honor demands or be told to do something by a person not in a position of authority. Next, the level of anger and disrespect displayed when your instructions aren't followed, especially when speaking of such trivial tasks as cleaning windows and mopping floors, is alarming, and to me, shows a deeper problem with the underlying issues of control and the need to feel listened to.

Tran took the cake when he re-mopped the entire main lobby area after I had already completed it. I'm not sure if he thought I hadn't done it correctly or if he was purposely being spiteful. Either way, he added an additional 25-30 minutes of us being in the lobby when we could be back in our units. I didn't say anything though, because if I objected, it would've made matters worse. This was only the second day on the job! All in all, I definitely feel that I handled myself well. I didn't allow his disrespectful comments to bait me in and extract a negative reaction. I remained calm and continued on with my work, despite his childish behavior. I'm a pretty reserved, laid back person overall. As a result, it takes a lot to anger me and bring me completely out of character.

However, if this is how working with this man will be each morning, this will act as the ultimate test of my patience and temperament. Once our work was complete, we were sent back to receiving, stripped searched, changed, and sent back to C-1.

While watching TV in the unit following the shift, I saw my cousin Curtis Holland III's face on the screen. It was on a public television network that was airing an old segment where a group called the Avid Achievers was interviewing him, along with 2 other top high school athletes. This interview occurred during Curtis's senior year of high school of 2017-2018. At that time, Curtis was heavily regarded as the best high school basketball player in Anne Arundel County, and one of the top throughout the state. He finished second in the vote for Anne Arundel County Player of the Year. He lost the award, but many people (including myself) feel that he was robbed of receiving this distinction. Since then, Curtis has received a full athletic scholarship to play basketball at High Point University in North Carolina, a Division I program. He successfully completed his first year (2018-2019) there where, as a freshman, he played quality minutes, even working his way into the starting lineup, and had his best performances against some the team's toughest matchups. In the interview, Curtis spoke about his college selection process, how he was happy with the selection he made, and the burden that earning a full scholarship took off of his family. Curtis is an extremely gifted ball player; among the best I've seen to come out of our small area in at least 15 years. He's equipped with all of the tools needed to make it professionally, whether in the states or overseas. All he has to do is continue to work and maintain the belief within himself that he can make it to the next level. At times, he can get down on himself, and it reflects in his mannerisms while on the court, and ultimately his play. But, he's still young, and as he matures, I think that this will be seen less and less. I, along with the rest of his family, am extremely proud of him, and can't wait to see where he'll allow the game to take him.

I was finally able to be taken up to the medical unit to get some more contact solution. The nurses there both initially said that they didn't have any, although I had been given some days prior in A-1 by another nurse. Next, they said they didn't know where it was kept. You would've thought I was asking for an early release by what I had to go through just so I wouldn't have dry, red eyes from not being able to soak my contacts.

I took my first shower in C-1 this morning. Since everyone else is at work when Tran and I return from our shifts, early morning presents the perfect opportunity to wash my ass with a little more privacy than usual.

This morning's breakfast consisted of a biscuit with sausage gravy, oatmeal, breakfast cake and chocolate milk. I didn't eat any of what was served.

After showering, I laid in bed. Martin is syndicated on many TV networks, including VH1, which they air in the wee hours of the morning. In this specific episode, Martin was sick, and Gina was attempting to tend to him while also trying to complete a work presentation by the submission deadline. When Martin told Gina that the sheets he was laying on were hurting him, I laughed almost uncontrollably. Then, after Martin's several unsuccessful requests for Gina to make him some chicken noodle soup, he said, "Fine, I'll just make my own soup. Since you didn't!" I laughed like it was my first time watching it, like I hadn't seen this episode 1,000 times. It's not so much of what he said, but the sickly, self-pity tone in which he made the statement gets me every time. Nothing else in the world mattered at that moment other than Martin having his chicken noodle soup made. This episode always reminds me of when Sammy, one of my closest friends, confirmed that he acts exactly like this when he's under the weather. I've seen every episode of Martin multiple times over, but I still watch and laugh at it like it's a new show that's airing. Classic show.

While sleeping, about 4 CO's came into C-1 around 7:30am to conduct a "shake down." They received word that someone in here had been making "hooch," or homemade alcohol. They removed Tran and I from the tier and placed us in a room next door for about 15 minutes while they proceeded to conduct a search of everyone's property. Once the search concluded, Tran and I were stripped search once more before returning. The CO's had ransacked the entire tier. Inmate mattresses were flipped over, sheets undone, and belongings had been tampered with without being restored back to their original positioning.

The CO's found a bottle of fruit and juice that was in the process of being turned into a prohibited beverage. Although this liquid hadn't fully made the transformation into alcohol, it was still considered contraband. The CO informed Tran and I that if no one confessed to the bottle being theirs, then all of C-1 would be on lock down for 24 hours, which means not having access to the TV or phones for that entire period. Tran and I were then asked if we knew whose bottle it was and we both denied having such information.

Of course, upon returning from work, none of the other inmates confessed to the substance being theirs, so we were placed on lock down, and our outdoor recreation time that we were supposed to have for Sunday was taken away. While putting their belongings back in order after the shake down, some of the inmates realized that some of their property, mainly clothing, was missing. Thankfully, none of my belongings were misplaced in the process.

The CO's even removed the sheets that were hanging in the bathroom area and used to create more privacy between the 2 toilets and the shower. Since I had an extra blue sheet, I gave it up to allow it to be used to re-create our "hut" for when someone needs to use the bathroom.

After that eventful morning, I sat and played Scrabble with a group of the guys while on lock down. They all could tell that it was my first time being locked up and that my charge was most likely for a DUI. They were surprised to hear that I received a job so quickly, but knew that it was most likely attributed to me not having a real criminal record and that I was minimal risk. I told them that I believed my persistence had a part to play as well. One of the inmates playing was also there for a DUI, for which he received a sentence of 120 days. Another inmate playing had been at JRDC since October 28th of 2018 awaiting trial. He was caught with 26 pounds of weed. I'm pretty certain that this wasn't for medicinal use, so I'm sure that he's going to have to fork out a good amount of money for his defense.

Today's lunch was red beans with meat and white rice, green beans, pineapples, and the cake-style bread. It's shaped like a cake, but not an actual cake, and it isn't cornbread. So, cake-style bread is the best way that I can describe it. I didn't eat any of it though. I had been snacking on some of the chocolate-chip cookies and crackers that I had in my commissary, so that should hold me over until dinner.

I read a book review in the Sunday Capital on Albert Woodfox's memoir entitled Solitary. Albert was a former member of the Black Panther Party that served a 50-year prison sentence for armed robbery. While serving this sentence, Albert was wrongfully convicted of the 1972 stabbing of a white prison guard and, as a result, was forced to serve more than 40 years in solitary confinement in Angola Prison (Louisiana State Penitentiary), the largest maximum-security prison in the United States. The time that Woodfox and Herman Wallace, another inmate convicted with Woodfox for the same crime, served in solitary confinement is known as the longest period of solitary confinement in American prison history. Robert King was convicted of a separate prison murder in 1973 and ended up serving 29 years in solitary confinement. His case was overturned, and he was released in 2001. These former inmates are now famously known as the "Angola 3." The U.S. Court of Appeals also eventually overturned Woodfox's conviction in 1974 in November of 2014. He was finally released in February of 2016, after the prosecution agreed to stop its pursuit of a retrial in exchange for Woodfox's plea to lesser charges. Woodfox still maintains his innocence and stated that he would've liked to prove it in court, but chose the plea deal instead due to his advanced age and deteriorating health.

Albert's memoir speaks about his life prior to imprisonment, the inhumane conditions and treatment he experienced during his time in Angola, and furthermore, calls for a thorough re-examination and reform of the criminal justice system as a whole, especially the experience one undergoes while in solitary confinement. Being that he emerged unbroken from such deplorable conditions, Albert's story is also a true testament to the strength of the human will and spirit. The fact that he was able to produce a memoir of nearly 500 pages, all while in solitary confinement is completely fascinating to me. Humans aren't made to be isolated in the manner that solitary confinement forces. It's literally designed to break you. On top of this, there is not a speck of inspiration to be found in solitary confinement; there isn't enough happening throughout the course of one's day to develop any interesting content. So, I can only imagine the level of depth Albert went within himself in order to have something valuable to produce. I definitely have to get my hands on this work once I'm out.

Also, in The Capital, there was an interesting story about a woman from West Baltimore who returned after fleeing from her mother's home at age 14, changing her name, and living in New York under a different alias for over 20 years. The woman had been raped repeatedly as a child, and thought her mother knew about it but refused to act. So rather than informing her mother of what happened, she just decided to leave, unbeknownst to her mother, and created a new identity in a new city. Although they ultimately reunited years later, this is a terrible story. I couldn't imagine the pain a parent experiences when their child vanishes, and there's no way of knowing where they could've gone, let alone where the parent should even begin looking to find them. On top of this, to learn the reason behind one's child leaving home was because he or she was being sexually assaulted, and thinking that you allowed it as the parent, is something from which I'm sure most parents would have a hard time recovering. I don't have any children, but I do understand the importance of maintaining an open line of communication with one's children, and ensuring they feel comfortable coming to the parent about any issues they may have. Additionally, being a little intrusive, or nosey, as a parent is something that I'm sure is off-putting to children, but it allows for parents to sense when something may be wrong in their child's life, and the work of addressing the issue can then begin. Asking questions, starting somewhat uncomfortable conversations, and reminding them that they can always seek the parent for guidance and/or advice are all ways that parents can remain informed of their child's endeavors, and take necessary precautions to attempt to create safer conditions so, hopefully, a story such as this can be avoided.

I also read in the paper that Maryland has the highest percentage of failed public housing inspections in the country, with D.C. as the only jurisdiction that did worse. I've been to Baltimore countless times throughout my life, and I've seen some of the public housing conditions there, so I'm not surprised by this statistic at all.

Dinner this evening was beans, and meat-in-a-ball that we inmates affectionately call "Rottweiler." The meat was bigger than an actual meatball, and nowhere near as tender. We also had a side cabbage, and a snack cake for dessert. I only ate the cabbage, along with a few crackers from my commissary. Dinner was essentially the same as lunch today, except for the meat was served by itself in a ball-like form instead of mixed in with the beans, and there wasn't any rice to mix.

After dinner, I winded down and got some rest before we were called for work. I tried listening to my radio again. It still doesn't get any reception. I'm not able to get any stations that I listen to normally. The only station that I received clearly was 99.9 WNAV, the local Annapolis station. It's a soft rock/oldies R&B station, so I managed with it. Also, on this same station, I kept hearing an advertisement being played about a book publishing company, Dorn's Publishing, and their number, 800-485-6904, kept being repeated. If I plan on publishing this memoir, I will need a publishing company in the future. Not saying that I'm going to use this company once I'm ready for publishing, but I definitely took this as a sign to not stop until my story is released. I more day down.

Monday, March 25th, 2019

Work was cool this morning. We started on time, around 1am, unlike yesterday where we weren't called out until around 1:30am. We started this morning's shift by cleaning a classroom on the 2nd floor where the CO's report for roll call. Tran swept and mopped the floor, and I washed all of the windows.

Tran and I worked well together this morning. There weren't any outbursts or attitudes from him or I. We switched responsibilities today, with him washing all of the windows and me sweeping and mopping the lobby and bathroom floors. After I mopped the first two thirds of the lobby area, Tran told me to take a break and he mopped the remaining area. He wasn't checking over my work or repeating the work that I already did, like he was doing yesterday. We finished around 3:20am.

Tomorrow is supposedly Tran's last day of work here in the lobby. I guess that he'll be stationed to work someplace else in the jail. I can't say that I'll be sad to see him go. I'll now be solely responsible for cleaning the lobby area each morning until my release date of April 13th. I have no problem with assuming this responsibility, especially with performing these types of duties.

I got back in bed immediately after returning from our shift. I didn't even bother getting up to see what was for breakfast.

The phone and TV were turned back on between 9 and 10am this morning, officially ending our 24-hour lock down stint. Being on lock down here was nowhere near as bad as when I was in A-1. At least in C-1, we had games to play to keep us occupied for that period. Each of us also had to leave the unit at some point to go to work, which lessened the time spent in the cell without TV or phone access.

I definitely made sure to call Moms and Ms. Elizabeth and tell them about my experience working with Tran yesterday morning. They both were in shock by his behavior, agreeing that it was totally uncalled for. They also reminded me that this position was only temporary and to not allow him to get me to a point where my position, and/or my freedom, would be further jeopardized. I couldn't agree with them more, as I already maintained this mentality.

In today's paper, I read that the report produced by special counsel Robert Mueller revealed that there was ultimately no collusion between President Trump, or any of his associates, with the Russian government. It stated that the report was only 4 pages long. I try to loosely follow politics to, if for no reason at all, just be aware of current issues if brought up in conversation. So, I would never claim to be the person from whom to gain better understanding of a political issue. But, I am almost certain when I say that no governmental report, especially one intended to defend this current administration from accusations of arguably the biggest conspiracy in American political history, can deem itself sufficient with only 4 pages. Most high school reports require more length and detail, so to not hold this same standard to our current government, who may have potentially received assistance from a foreign entity to manipulate our most recent presidential election, is absolutely ridiculous. I'm sure this isn't the last to be heard about this report.

I also read that Rob Gronkowski, "The Gronk," is retiring from the NFL after 9 seasons of playing tight end for the New England Patriots. Gronk, although relatively short, had a very decorated career in the NFL, including 5 Pro Bowl appearances, 4 First Team All Pro selections, and most importantly, helping the Patriots win 3 of their 6 Super Bowls. He battled extremely tough injuries throughout his career that took their toll on his body and forced him to retire probably earlier than he wanted. But, even with a shorter career than other greats at his position, Gronk is still regarded by many football analysts as being the best tight end in NFL history. There's no doubt that Gronk will be a first ballot Hall of Famer, equipped with a gold jacket with a sculpture of his face enshrined in Canton, Ohio.

I'm late, but I finally figured out the jail's phone system today. When using the phone here, there are two options that one can select. By pressing 1 at the beginning of a call, I was electing to use money from my own commissary account to talk on the phone. This was for speaking to people on the outside that did not have accounts established to speak to inmates. Phone time, just like everything else outside of what is issued to an inmate, is purchased when an inmate makes their commissary order. It must be purchased by the end of Wednesday in order for it to be active by Saturday. But, if I pressed 0, the money was coming out of a phone account that the person I was calling already had established. There were times prior to today when I would attempt to make calls to either my mother or Ms. Elizabeth but was unable to connect, when they had already confirmed having phone accounts established in order to accept my calls. This was because I was selecting option 1, and I had not yet purchased any phone time. I'm glad I finally was able to get this squared away.

There was a verbal altercation this afternoon over the TV, as 2 inmates wanted to watch 2 different things. An argument ensued, voices got loud, but ultimately, nothing happened. The argument was quickly squashed and both guys dapped one another as to indicate a peaceful end to a brief disagreement.

Lunch was sausage (I think), cabbage, macaroni salad, bread, and a snickerdoodle cookie. I only ate the cabbage, macaroni salad, and the cookie.

After lunch, we were allowed to go up to the library. We were given an hour to read, research, and check out materials. We were allowed to check out up to 2 books at a time but weren't permitted to check out any magazines. I ended up checking out former (but forever) President Barack Obama's The Audacity of Hope. Barack wrote this book in 2006 while serving in the Illinois state senate, prior to becoming President of the United States. I always heard and read reviews that praised this book. It was a NY time's bestseller, and Obama was one of the best orators we had to head this nation, so I'm sure his literary work will prove just as great.

I witnessed a group of the guys make a "hook-up" for the first time today. A hook-up is essentially a jailhouse meal comprised of a number of different ingredients from an inmate's commissary. It can be made in several different ways using various components. Ramen noodles usually serve as the base for this dish. I watched as one of the inmates whipped one big meal for several of the others. He wore plastic gloves while crafting this jailhouse delicacy, just as you'd see an employee behind the counter at Subway making sandwiches. He crushed several noodles packets down to a rice form and poured them into a clear trash bag. He then poured hot water from the shower into the trash bag in order to cook the rice, mixing the bag all around to ensure that the water was distributed evenly through each broken noodle. There were a few packets of cheese sauce that he mixed with crunched Cheetos and a little water. Then, using his jail ID, he chopped up various commissary items, including dill pickles, artificial jalapenos, mackerel fillets (a type of packaged fish), sausages, peeled eggs, and crushed potato chips. Once he felt the crushed noodles were finished cooking, he drained the excess water, and added all of these ingredients into the trash bag with the crushed noodles/rice and resumed mixing. After the mixing process was complete, and using a cup as a serving utensil, he dipped it into the bag and began filling each bowl with this newly concocted dish. He'd put a portion in the bowl, then layer it with the cheese mix, and continued to do this in each bowl until the trash bag was empty, and all of the bowls were full. The serving was enough to completely fill about 6 bowls.

I was definitely intrigued from watching the making of this meal. First, by the ingredients, as I'm sure that none of what was mixed together to create this hook-up would be things that any of these guys would eat on the outside, well at least I wouldn't. Along with the elements of this dish, I was also just as in awe by the care and efficiency with which it was made. This isn't said to be insulting or at all belittling, but I could tell that the particular inmate who crafted this dish had experience with making it. From the gloves worn, to the way that he twirled the trash bag of crushed noodles, to the preciseness with which he chopped the ingredients, and the way he evenly distributed the finished product, one could conclude that he was well-seasoned in cheffing up this meal.

I played Scrabble again with one of the other guys from the game on Sunday. The same guy from Sunday's contest won this one as well. He's a wordsmith. I enjoy the game of Scrabble. Although I do like to win, I play the game more for the opportunity to be educated, as I love learning new words and potentially expanding my vocabulary.

Dinner this evening was turkey, mashed potatoes, pineapples and bread. A vegetable was also served, but I was unsure as to what it actually was. I only ate the pieces of turkey, some of the mashed potatoes, and the pineapples.

I chilled out for the remainder of the evening, read some more of Obama's book, and got some rest before being called for work. 1 more down.

Tuesday, March 26th, 2019

This morning's shift went well, until it neared the end. I washed all of the windows, and did a portion of the sweeping, while Tran mopped.

While Tran was mopping, there were some individuals standing outside of the main entrance, appearing as if one of them came to turn themselves in. They were knocking on the glass to get our attention. Being that Tran was closer to the control desk where the CO's sat, I asked him to notify the CO of these individuals. A simple request, or so I thought. Tran thought otherwise. He stated that he wasn't going to do this because it wasn't a part of his job, and that I should notify the CO myself if I wanted them to have this information. He then proceeded to shoo me away like I was a pet or something, then had the nerve to call me lazy. I wanted to curse his ass out, but I know there'd be no benefit in it for me, as his attitude would still remain as it had been.

I notified the CO of the individuals standing outside of the front entrance, and he stated that he had already seen them on camera. He then "suggested" that I make myself look busy because it looked like I was just standing around on camera. I'm sure that this was the perception, but it was because I completed my tasks for the night and was waiting on Tran's slow ass to complete his. Everything had already been finished, and all that needed to be done was mopping, Tran's responsibility. It isn't my fault that he doesn't complete his tasks as quickly as I do mine. I've never been 1 for busy work, or creating the illusion of appearing busy in order to appease someone else, especially with cleaning this lobby. It's obvious that there already isn't enough work here to keep 2 people consistently busy, so to now be expected to look busy, while there's no one even around to look busy for, is completely asinine. And, of course, Tran decided to re-mop a section that he finished earlier. I guess I'm expected to still appear busy and wait while my stubborn, childish, co-worker finishes duplicating work as well.

It was also informed to me that Trans last day working here wouldn't be today, but he would remain working here until his release on April 9th; which means, I'll have to put up with him and his childish attitude for the next 2 weeks.

Although being without my freedom is trying in itself, the real test of my character and patience is having to work with this character for the remaining weeks until his release. He is stubborn, incompetent, childish, and completely lacks the ability to reason; an all-around asshole. Working with him is only, at most, 2 and a half hours of my day, so I can and will withstand him as a co-worker for the sake of an earlier release. However, I know that being silent while he carries on this way will become increasingly more difficult for me. I don't know anyone who would continuously take someone cursing and talking down to them, especially without valid reason.

Breakfast was grits, potatoes, what appeared to be an egg-type quiche, and chocolate milk. I didn't eat any of it. I laid down and rested/slept until lunch.

For lunch, we had meatballs with rice and gravy, broccoli, bread, and 2 snickerdoodle cookies. I ate most of the meatballs, rice and broccoli.

In today's paper, I read that Apple is starting a new streaming TV service, Apple TV + (Plus). It's planned to release this fall and will feature original shows and movies across every genre. Sounds like more competition will be added to the newly booming streaming service wave. The company also is launching its own credit card, called the Apple Card, which will be designed to primarily use with Apple Pay on various Apple devices. It's scheduled to be released sometime this summer.

I then read that there was a shooting and stabbing at My Place Bar and Lounge in Odenton, Md. over the weekend. I haven't been to this particular spot, but I've known a few people who've frequented there, and I've heard some of the stories. Several violent altercations have taken place here over the years. My cousin's ex-husband was shot in the parking lot here some years ago, so I'm not surprised to hear that something else like that has happened. I hope everyone involved is alright.

Dinner this evening was spaghetti, carrots, pineapples, and bread. I didn't eat any of what was served, just snacked on a few crackers from my commissary.

I watched as 2 guys worked out this evening. All calisthenics work; push-ups, pull-ups, and dips. Each of them were already pretty cut. They reminded me that I need to get back into a consistent gym regimen once I leave here because I've been slacking. The pull-up bar hangs right beside my bed too. I should start making use of it.

This evening, I spoke on the phone some, and continued reading the work of former President Obama. Before you know it, it was time to lay it down, as the morning, and work, would soon be approaching. Another day down.

Wednesday, March 27th, 2019

Work started off rocky this morning, as Tran initially was on his regular bullshit. But, once things started getting underway, the shift ended up going smoothly. We didn't speak to one another again this morning, and again I was completely fine with this. I did the windows along with the trash, and Tran swept and mopped.

Tran, once again, re-mopped the entire lobby area. I think he does this to keep busy while we wait for a CO to let us back into the supply closet to return the materials. This is the only justification that I find. Once we've completed our task, Tran doesn't like going to the control desk to inform one of the CO's that we're finished. I guess he feels that we'd be asking them to do too much, even though they aren't doing much of anything overnight anyways. Rather, he waits until a CO is coming in on their shift, or leaving to go outside on a break, and asks them to open the door to the supply closet. There is no set time for this, so it inevitably keeps us out in the lobby waiting longer than necessary, along with the additional time we must wait to be let back into receiving to be searched. I'd say that, all in all, our work shift consists of an hour and a half of actual work, with an additional 30 to 45 minutes added waiting. The extra time allocated solely to waiting could be spent back in C-1 sleeping.

This morning's breakfast was pancakes, oatmeal, a single slice of bologna, and chocolate milk. I didn't eat anything. Instead, I laid in my bed and went to sleep.

Once I woke back up later in the morning, a CO came around and gave me the results from my blood test taken on the 20th. I tested negative for HIV, Hepatitis C, and Syphilis. I was very confident that the results would come back negative, but whenever being tested for a sexually transmitted disease, one can never be fully at ease until confirmation is received.

Not too much long after, Ms. Kellie retrieved me and brought me up with her to a room on the second floor to conduct an exit interview. It's jail policy that an exit interview is conducted with each inmate within 30 days of their release. It felt a little soon, being that I had only been here for about 2 weeks and I was already having an exit interview, but that's just the timing of my sentence.

She asked some general questions, but also asked about what I plan to do to not come back to jail again, as well as identifying some of jail's positive and negative aspects. I told her that my plan for remaining free was to, essentially, do what I've been continually doing in terms of living a productive life; continue going to work, continue to pay my bills in a timely manner, continue to travel, and continue to have positive interactions with others and maintain positive relationships with my support system. The only thing that I would change would be to, obviously, make smarter decisions and to be more responsible about driving whenever alcohol is involved.

Being that I am an individual that tries to identify optimism in any situation, I informed Ms. Kellie that there are a few positive things that I've taken thus far from this experience. First, if you weren't, prior to arriving, jail will instill humility. I've always viewed myself as a humble person who appreciates all of the possessions I've attained, and opportunities I've been granted throughout my life. I've always remained cognizant that the space in life where I find myself currently, the places I've been fortunate to see, and the feats I've been able to accomplish would never have been possible if not for the love, support, and investment from others. However, when stripped of these things, and all of the amenities to which I have daily access and treated without the esteem that I may customarily garner, it's a reminder of how much more appreciative I could always be. In here, you are treated just as everyone else. Financial status, possessions, or job title are all irrelevant, and you are forced to coexist and interact with people that you may not do so under normal circumstances. In here, the character of a person is what holds the most weight; how you speak to and treat others, manners, being considerate and respectful. These things can be easily clouded by one's lifestyle and status when on the outside. However, these same features are even more heightened when here, as failure to be mindful of them during your stay could have grave consequences.

Second, if nothing else, jail gives you time to think, strategize, and lay a blueprint for your next endeavor whenever you're released. It gives you an opportunity to really reflect on your misstep, the measures you will take in the future to ensure that you never find yourself in the same position, and to map out, in detail, a plan of action to put in motion upon your release.

One comment that Ms. Kellie made during my interview stood out to me. While we were discussing what I do for a living and my plans upon my release, she stated, "It sounds like you had a pretty good life before you came here." I quickly corrected her by stating, "No, I have a pretty good life currently." "Had" indicated that the life I'd built for myself was a thing of the past, when, fortunately, this is not at all the case. Although my current condition is not the greatest, my life as a whole is still great overall. And, fortunately when released, I will still be able to come home to the same quality of life that I possessed prior to me turning myself in. I know that many inmates, due to the length of time spent in jail, are not able to maintain their previous quality of life. For this, I am extremely thankful.

In today's Capital, there was a write up about a double shooting in Glen Burnie Monday night in the Tall Pines apartments. Also, the charges were dropped on the suspect in the double homicide that took place in the 300 block of Highland Dr. in Glen Burnie from Sunday, March 24th. Glen Burnie has been extremely hot recently.

Also, there was a man found with 53 guns in his truck while at a DUI stop on Route 3/Crain Highway in Bowie this past Monday. Having that amount of artillery on a person at once is crazy.

Since the beginning of my stay here, I've usually only read the Capital, but I picked up The Baltimore Sun today. In their sports section, they had a front-page article on Phil Booth, the senior guard from Villanova. He's a Baltimore native. The article spoke about his successful collegiate basketball career at Villanova, the value and leadership he brought to the team, and the overall positive impact he'll be leaving on the program at the end of his final season. He's projected to go mid to late 2nd round in the 2019 NBA Draft. I've made it a point to try and follow Phil over the past couple of college basketball seasons because I went to college with his sister, Jazmin Watkins-Booth. Although she is a few years younger, we both attended Howard at the same time. We both were even apart of the same social organization while there, Campus Pals.

For lunch, we had Sloppy Joe sandwiches, potatoes, green beans, and yellow cake with icing. I only ate the potatoes and the green beans.

I rapped briefly with the guy who was caught with 26 pounds of weed, and he told me more information in reference to his case. He said that police raided his house on October 9th from an "anonymous tip" they received, which is how they were able to get a search warrant. He stated that he is facing a minimum of 18 months, but a maximum of 5 years. He's been in here since October, and will most likely be in until at least June, the month of his court date. His attorney is John Robinson, who is one of the best criminal defense attorneys in the state. He stated that John was going to attempt to have the police search warrant suppressed entirely, as an anonymous tip is hearsay, and not sufficient enough grounds for a search warrant to be issued. If his lawyer is able to do this, then his case could be thrown out altogether. Since being in here, he stated that his girl has been sticking by his side, and orders commissary for him on a weekly basis. However, he does have a 3-year-old son that he misses. All I can do is wish him the best outcome with his situation, because it definitely sounds like he's fighting an uphill battle.

At 2:30pm this afternoon, we went outside for recreation time. It definitely felt good to see the sunshine and breathe fresh air. Our rec area was a half court black top area with one basketball goal without a net, and 2 workout machines that looked more like Fisher Price toys.

I played a friendly game of 50 with one of the other inmates (I won) and got to hear a little about his story. He was a short and stocky white guy, age 27. I never caught his real name, but the other guys in the unit affectionately call him "Billy Bob." He said that he received juvenile life in the state of Pennsylvania at age 13 for stealing 17 cars in one night, and racking up a total of 27 felonies as a result back in 2006. 17 cars in one night has to be some type of record. I don't think they stole that many cars altogether in the urban classic film New Jersey Drive.

I'm not sure of how juvenile life works, because I'd assume that he'd be in jail in PA serving this sentence. However, he stated that he's actually on the run from PA, and that he doesn't think that state is aware of the new charges he's caught down here. He's been in JRDC since July of 2018. He was initially charged with 2 first degree assaults. Through a plea deal arrangement, the state wanted to give him 20 years, suspending all but 8. Instead, he decided to take it to trial, and he actually made out better than if he accepted the state's original deal. He ended up having the 2 1st degree assault charges reduced to 2nd degree assault. He is now waiting to be sentenced, which is scheduled for April 10th.

Dinner was served about an hour and a half after we returned from rec time. We had bologna topped with a cream sauce and sliced potatoes, sweet potatoes, pineapples, and bread. Cream sauce on a bologna slice is not in any way appetizing, so I didn't touch that at all. I ate a few of the sliced potatoes with cream sauce, all of the sweet potatoes, and all of the pineapples.

Ms. Elizabeth visited me again this evening. We've spoken everyday on the phone since I've been here, but it's always good whenever I get to see her face, even if through a glass. She keeps me updated on all that's been going on in pop culture while I've been away, as there's something new occurring daily. We talk about how our workdays were, and about any new stories we've heard or encounters we've had. A quality visit indeed.

Moms let me know that she still hasn't seen any mail or e-mails sent to me from my job regarding my reinstatement. No news is still good news at this point. She also made me aware that NaNa, my grandmother, now knows that I'm in here. I purposely didn't tell her, and I also instructed my Mother not to say anything because I didn't' want her to worry herself sick with anticipation of me having to go and do time. I should've known though that being from a small town like Shady Side, where all of the black folks know one another, if not related, it was only a matter of time before word would get back to her. My grandmother and I are very close, as I was one of her only grandchildren to actually live with her for a big portion of my upbringing. Due to this, we share a special attachment to one another. I had every intent of notifying her, but I wanted to do so after being released, so that the feelings of worry and fear that would come with her knowing about my incarceration would not be present, as that time would have already passed. I told my mother that I'd call and speak to her while I was in here.

2 new guys moved into the unit tonight. Both will be working in the kitchen as well. One of them, due to health reasons I'm assuming, was required to have a bottom bunk, meaning one of the inmates had to move to a top bunk in order to accommodate the new inmate. This was not a favorable move, as the bottom bunks are the most sought after, but there was no other alternative. I'm already on the top bunk, so I wasn't affected.

Some of the guys made another "hook-up" again tonight with all of the ingredients from when I first witnessed it being made. Still intriguing to me, but still not enough to want to taste for myself.

Prior to winding down for the evening, I caught the last bit of School Daze on BET. Spike Lee, the film's director, tackles the issues of colorism and classism in the African American community told through the lens of black college students attending a fictional HBCU. Forever a classic. I remember, as a Campus Pal at Howard, we would show this movie on the Yard for the incoming freshmen during Freshmen Week. I can tell that many of the guys hadn't seen this movie though. And most of them definitely didn't understand the "WAKE UP!" sequence at the end, arguably the most memorable part of the movie.

The Lakers lost to Denver by 15, 115-100.

I laid back for the rest of the evening, continued to read more of The Audacity of Hope, and got some rest until we were called for work early the next morning. 1 more day in the books.

Thursday, March 28th, 2019

Work went well this morning. Tran stated that we should try to work a little slower. I'm assuming that he doesn't want to work too fast in fear of being given additional tasks to complete. He stated this is the reason that he re-mops the floor almost every morning. I still don't agree with this action, as there isn't even anyone out here with us in the morning to delegate more tasks, but at least I now understand his reasoning. He mopped again this morning, and I did the windows, trash, and some of the sweeping. We were actually finished around 2:30am this morning, but after Tran re-mopping, waiting for a CO to let us back into the supply closet, and then being processed in the receiving unit, it tacked on another hour and a half to our workday. We were back in C-1 around 3:45am.

While waiting in the lobby for a CO to come, Tran and I actually spoke, and I learned about him outside of the asshole that I encountered the first few days on the job. Contrary to what I originally thought, Tran is actually Vietnamese. He's been in the U.S. for about 33 years, as he came here in 1986 at the age of 19. He lives on the eastern shore in the Stevensville area, and works as a mechanic at the Toyota dealership on West St. in Annapolis. He has 2 daughters, ages 17 and 23. The youngest is a junior in high school, while the oldest is a University of Maryland graduate, and is currently attaining her business law degree from a college in Pennsylvania. He stated that he is proud of them both. He last visited his home country about 15 years ago. He stated that all of his family is now here in the states. They are spread between MD/DC, Virginia and Cali. His birthday is also approaching, as he will turn 52 on April 1st.

Breakfast this morning was a biscuit and sausage gravy, grits, cornbread (I believe), and chocolate milk. I didn't eat any of it.

In today's paper, I read that Governor Hogan plans to veto a $15 per hour minimum wage spending bill. I'm sure this won't go over to well with service industry and food service workers on their quests for livable wages. As wages increase, inevitably so will the cost of goods. However, I do believe that there needs to be an increase to our minimum wage, as the cost of living in Md. is among the highest in the nation and continues to rise.

The police are still searching for the young couple that are suspects in the double homicide that occurred in Glen Burnie this past Sunday (3/24/19). The couple is from Brooklyn Park, the northernmost part of Anne Arundel County.

Jay Jalisi, a delegate of Baltimore County, was reprimanded by fellow lawmakers for demeaning behavior towards staff.

A male Navy Midshipmen is currently awaiting trial for an alleged sexual assault that occurred in Pensacola, Fla. in March of 2018 involving a female Navy reservist. This Midshipmen is white, young, respected, and very well accomplished within the Navy program, so it will be interesting to see the outcome of this case.

There were record graduation rates in Anne Arundel County in 2018, but the achievement gap has widened slightly, the most it has been since 2014.

In the sports section, I read that Maryland Terrapins running back Ty Johnson clocked a 4.26 in the 40-yard dash, according to social media reports, at the Maryland Pro Day. If this was ran at the NFL combine, it would've been the fastest time recorded at the combine that year, and among the fastest times recorded in combine history. A lot of players have earned NFL contracts from running slower 40-yard dash times, so this is indeed impressive.

The Naval Academy will begin a new 12-year contract with the AAC (American Athletic Conference) that is set to begin during the 2020-2021 school year. The deal is reportedly worth $1 billion.

For lunch, we had a slice of bologna with circular tortilla chips, a side salad, cake with icing, and bread. I only ate the tortilla chips.

I spoke to my man Bush and Ms. Elizabeth again this evening via phone. Ms. Elizabeth told me that WOW airlines, an Iceland based airline service known for offering very affordable flights to Europe, abruptly went out of business; so abruptly that they discontinued transportation for trips that were currently in progress! This is definitely unfortunate, as I love to travel, and probably would've ended up flying WOW for a trip to a European country in the future.

Dinner this evening was Salisbury steak with mashed potatoes and gravy, broccoli, bread, and honeydew melon. I ate all of the steak, some of the mashed potatoes, and all of the melon.

I watched a couple of the guys do a calisthenics workout again. There are 3 inmates in my unit who are super cut. All push-ups and dips. Definitely need to get back to my gym routine once I get out. Summer is right around the corner.

I watched as an inmate put himself together a "hook-up" with some of his commissary ingredients. I asked one of the guys what a hook up actually tasted like. He said that it tasted good, but only while in here. He emphasized that it was strictly "some jail shit," and that it wouldn't taste good anyplace else. Duly noted.

BET had some good movies playing tonight. First, we watched 50 Cent's movie Get Rich or Die Tryin.' After watching 50 beat the odds to blow up as a rap superstar in this movie, you don't have a pulse if you don't walk away motivated.

Then afterwards, one of my all-time favorites came on, Above the Rim. This movie epitomized the mid 90's era, from the music, to the environment in NYC (where the movie was shot) at the time, and the feel as a whole. You knew 2Pac was a star after watching this movie, if you hadn't already. He was magnetic. The opening scene, where he walked in the gym with his crew to watch the ending of Kyle Lee Watson's high school game, was absolutely classic. He didn't even say anything, but you just knew he was the coolest, most important person in the gym at that moment. I may be in jail, but all felt almost right with the world while one of my favorite flicks was playing.

Once the movie went off, there was only 2 more hours until we were called for work. I rested and waited for the CO to come around. Another day down.

Friday, March 29th, 2019

We weren't retrieved for work until about 1:30am this morning, . But, work went smoothly again this morning, nonetheless. I did the trash, windows, and some of the sweeping. Tran also swept and did the mopping. After we were complete, we had to wait 40 more minutes until we were able to go back to receiving. The waiting is really the most strenuous part of this job.

When breakfast came around, I didn't even bother getting up to see what it was. I slept until about lunch time.

For lunch, we had tortilla chips (nachos) with meat, cheese sauce, corn, rice and beans, and honeydew melon. I ate the chips, meat, some of the corn, and all of the melon.

Not much longer after lunch, I was called out by a CO to come outside with the day shift MIO to help unload trash and recyclables that needed to be put in the trash compactor and big recycling bin. Prior to this, I didn't know that there was a daytime MIO. This MIO works upstairs where the assistant warden and facilities supervisor offices are housed.

These additional tasks didn't take long at all to complete, and it allowed me to go outside and gain some fresh air, so I had no complaints.

Coming back in from helping with the trash outside, I ran into one of the inmates from when I was in A1 as he was being released. I gave him a dap and told him to simply "stay out." His mother and his lady came to get him, and they all looked happy to be reunited with one another. He had a big smile on his face as he exited. I can't wait for this to be me in a few more weeks.

The guy that got caught with 26 pounds of grass was moved from C1 to a different unit today because he was fired from his job in the kitchen. Apparently, from what I was told, the kitchen hired a new supervisor, and he and the inmate got into a heated exchange. The inmate lost his cool, cursed the supervisor out, and was fired as a result.

I don't know this guy at all, but from my brief prior conversations with him, he gave off the impression that he is accustomed to being the smartest person in the room . And we all know that whenever someone begins a new job, there is a necessary learning curve that's needed. So, when a new supervisor began giving orders, especially when he may not have been completely familiar with his position and the daily regimen of the kitchen, I'm sure that's when miscommunication between he and the inmate began.

The girl who was in the paper a few days ago for being charged with a double homicide, along with her boyfriend, for the killing of the 2 men in Glen Burnie, was brought into JRDC today. In order to get to the female units, she had to be escorted right past our unit, so all of the guys saw her and knew immediately who she was. She is only 18, according to the paper. Definitely will try to follow this story closely.

I played 2 games of Scrabble today. I lost the first and won the second. I finally was able to beat the older guy who's been busting my ass. He's a wordsmith and is great with letter placement to help him earn big points for his words. In Scrabble, it's more about where the letters are placed on the board than the number of letters used. I ate a bag of mini cookies while I was playing.

Another inmate moved into our unit today. He, along with the guy that moved in yesterday, are both very talented drawers. They both kept books of sketches they'd done.

Dinner this evening was baked chicken and rice, vegetables, and pineapples. The chicken was actually good. I ate the entire meal, except for a little bit of the rice and the white bread (which is served with every meal, and I never eat). I can confidently say that I would've eaten this meal on the outside. I'll put this alongside the turkey and rice stir-fry style dish I had a few days ago as being the best meals I've had since the beginning of my stay.

In today's Capital, I read that lawmakers overrode Hogan's veto of $15 per hour minimum wage pay, as I was pretty sure that they would.

There are over 500 South River High School students that will have to retake the SAT test due to the fire alarm going off during their test taking time. This test already is nerve wracking and causes added anxiety and stress on these young students, as they prepare for months to take it, all with their futures in the balance. Now, they have to undergo these feelings again?! I understand safety is the first priority, but I'd be heated if I were one of these students. Best of luck to all of them.

Jay-Z (the G.O.A.T.) is going to receive the President's Award at the 50th Annual NAACP Image Awards. Very well deserving, and not just for his incredible music career, but for his public service and the fight for social justice for which he has been using his large platform over recent years. Salute to the big homey Hova.

In the sports section, there was a big article about former Annapolis Area Christian School graduate Taylor Murray finishing 17th all-time in scoring for the University of Kentucky program. I don't follow too much college women's hoops, but this is most definitely an awesome achievement, especially for someone coming from such a small area like this. I'm sure that she'll be going to the next level, whether the WNBA or overseas. I wish her nothing but success as she takes that step.

Some of the guys made another "hook-up" tonight, but it was a much smaller portion.

I noticed that time seemed to go by pretty fast today. Between helping with the trash outside, the 2 back-to-back games of Scrabble, and VH1 playing good flicks one after another (Set It Off, Menace II Society and Notorious), nighttime came quicker than usual.

I spoke to Moms again tonight. There still wasn't any word from my job pertaining to my reinstatement. There also hadn't been any emails from my union representative.

I snacked on my last bag of nacho chips as I watched Auburn beat UNC, 97-80. A few of my homeboys are UNC fans, so I know that they're sitting somewhere disgusted after watching the Tar Heel performance. The Tigers are now headed to the Elite 8 of the NCAA tournament.

Duke beat Virginia Tech by 2, off a missed layup opportunity. Blue Devils are also headed to the Elite 8 of The Big Dance.

I took it down after the games. Work in the AM. 1 more day crossed off the calendar.

Saturday, March 30th, 2019

This morning was the best day of work yet, because no work was done. As Tran and I were at the supply closet about to retrieve our materials, the CO who walked us to the lobby received a call. He was told that the MIO's were to return to the unit, as the jail had suddenly been put on lockdown because an inmate had to be sent to the hospital. Due to this, Tran and I did not work, but were still credited as having worked today. The other overnight workers had to return to their units as well and would not be released until after breakfast was served.

Again, I stayed in bed when breakfast came around this morning. I didn't eat any of it.

Later in the morning, probably between 8-9am, Moms and Aunt Nisey came up to visit me. It was great to see them both. Aunt Nisey has always been there for me, and has always supported me, along with anyone in our family whenever they are in need. She bends over backwards for all of her children, brothers, sisters, nieces and nephews. She may be the most selfless person I know.

During the visit, we talked about how my experience was going thus far, my job while in here, and also about what had been occurring on the outside. My mother didn't know too much about the shootings that had recently taken place in Glen Burnie, but Aunt Nisey was well aware. She keeps her ear to the street. Also, all of her children and grandchildren currently live in the Glen Burnie area, especially her son, my cousin Andrew, who lives right around the corner from where one of the shootings took place. So, we spoke about these incidents, and also told past stories and shared some laughs.

Aunt Nisey made 2 powerful statements during this visit that really stuck with me. However, it wasn't just what she said, but more so how she said it. When she learned that I didn't tell NaNa about me having to do jail time prior to me turning myself in, she completely understood my explanation. But, she then stated, "You know, that woman is a lot stronger than y'all think." My grandmother raised 9 children, 6 of which of were boys. And most of her boys have had their individual struggles, some with drugs, alcohol, and other harder substances. Along with other grandchildren who have been in trouble and have had to serve time in jail. So, my situation is definitely not the first bit of adversity brought to the family. She made a very valid point with this statement.

Secondly, in reference to my current situation, she said something that I thought to be profound. Her words were not at all judgmental. She spoke in a calm, matter-of-fact like tone. "Because you know baby, it only gets worse from here." This resonated so deeply with me. She was telling the absolute truth. Prior to that statement, I hadn't thought much about how harsh the next consequence could be, but only the measures I needed to take to never find myself in this predicament ever again. But, Aunt Nisey's words made me think about the kind of example that the legal system would make of me if I got in trouble once more for this same thing. That next punishment, if I ever found myself here again, I may not be as equipped to endure. This was a scary thought, but a thought that needed to be planted in my brain.

"You know what they say about icebergs," she went on. "You can only see the top, but there's so much more at the bottom." Meaning that, if I found myself in trouble again, what I've endured thus far from my current situation would only be the surface of the hardships I'd have to undergo if there were a next time. I internalized what she said in those moments. Sometimes, the smallest statements have the hugest impact, all due to when, where, and how the message was delivered. This was a prime example of one of those instances. Aunt Nisey's statements greatly impacted me this day, more than she may ever know.

Commissary orders were delivered to us this morning. I ordered 3 pairs of medium size boxers (they only have white boxers as an option, no briefs), 2 small boxes of Frosted Flakes, 2 beef and cheese sticks, and another $25 worth of phone time that was added to my account. I ate both of the beef and cheese sticks as soon as I got them since I didn't eat breakfast.

I also received some mail today, which, again, caught me by surprise. Ms. Elizabeth wrote me a letter. She also printed some pictures from my Instagram, as well as from some of the trips we've taken together.

The letter had already been opened, as telling by the corners of the envelope that were already sliced open. The CO's go through all of the mail received at JRDC to ensure no contraband is attempting to be snuck in. The letter was dated on March 20th though, and I am just now receiving it on the 30th. As an estimate, let's say that the letter arrived to JRDC on March 22nd, and that's being generous. It still took an additional 8 days for me to receive the letter after the jail investigated its contents. If standard policy at JRDC is to have inmates waiting nearly 2 weeks after their mail arrives for them to receive it, that's a little unreasonable in my opinion. But, as with anything that goes on in here, there's little to nothing I can do to change the situation. I was very happy to receive my mail, nonetheless.

Once I got the letter, I called Ms. Elizabeth and told her that I had just received it. She was just as surprised as I am to hear that it had just gotten to me.

Today's lunch was hot dogs, rice and veggies, and honeydew melon. I only ate the rice and melon.

I played another game of Scrabble with the wordsmith and got dogged.

Middays during Saturdays are pretty quiet and boring, even more so than through the week it feels like.

I continued on with reading more of Audacity of Hope. I've made sure to read some of it each day since I checked it out. My goal is to have it completed prior to my release.

Dinner this evening was macaroni noodles and meat (Hamburger Helper style, but not that actual brand), green beans, bread, and a cookie. I ate a good portion of the main dish, all of the green beans, the cookie, and a cup of the green sugary juice. The hamburger meat was decently seasoned.

Some of the guys made another hook-up tonight.

I spoke to my cousin Andrew for the first time since being in here. We spoke for about an hour. It felt good to finally speak with my dawg. I told him about my experience in here thus far. We also spoke about the recent shootings that had been happening in Glen Burnie not far from where he lives. He stated that he wants to move from that area as soon as he can, as he would like to live in a safer area so that he doesn't have to worry about his son playing outside.

2 of the guys (the super cut-up ones), got into a verbal altercation tonight over the TV. One of the inmates wanted to watch the UFC fights that came on at 7pm on ESPN. He announced this earlier in the day to make sure no one objected, and he allowed for everyone else to watch what they wanted throughout the day. Once 7pm arrived, the other inmate stated that they weren't yet finished watching whatever was on, and that UFC would be turned on once whatever was being shown at the time was complete. A somewhat heated exchange ensued, but it was squashed quickly thereafter.

We spent the remainder of the evening watching the UFC fights. There were some NCAA basketball tournament games on also, but it was cool. I'm sure I'd get updated on the outcomes on the news and in the paper tomorrow. I guess I could live without watching hoop for an evening...I guess. Another day down.

Sunday, March 31st, 2019

Work went smoothly again this morning. Tran and I's work relationship seems to have gotten a lot better than when I initially started.

The CO that was in the control room, the same one from a few days ago who told me that I need to look busier, instructed me to clean the top of the lockers in the lobby this morning. This is something I've never done, nor ever been asked to do by any CO working in the control room overnight. Honestly, those CO's working in the control room during our shift could care less what we're doing. It's not like they go behind us and check our work after we're finished. This particular guard already had the image of me not appearing busy enough from a few days prior, so he felt the need to give me something additional to do. Just flexing his muscle for the sake of doing so. I had no other choice in the matter, so I did what I was told.

Breakfast was cereal, pineapples, coffee cake, cornbread, and sausage. I ate the Frosted Flakes from my commissary, the pineapples, and the coffee cake.

It was our unit's turn for rec time this morning. I stayed asleep while some of the other guys went out.

In today's Capital, I read that the city of Annapolis is suing the opioid industry for $400 million. The lawsuit names some of the biggest pharmaceutical companies in the nation as taking part in a campaign to obscure the dangers of opioids, all the while continuing to promote them as safe and/or necessary.

The country as a whole, including this small area of Anne Arundel County, has been hit hard by opioid addiction and death within recent years. Due to this, law enforcement and medical professionals have been taking additional measures to attempt to address this issue. While I am all for addressing the opioid crisis in our country, and saving as many lives as possible, it's hard to overlook that this same attention was not brought to the crack cocaine epidemic that spread throughout nearly ever inner city, and predominantly black neighborhoods, in the country during the 80's.

Opioid addiction has, historically, been more of a presence in the white community. Now that the addiction and death rates from opioids have recently heightened, it's gained national attention, and more resources have been allocated to help those who've become addicted. However, the same life vests weren't thrown to black folks when they fell victim to the potency of crack cocaine. They weren't labeled as addicts who needed treatment, but instead, criminals who needed to be removed from the streets and thrown in jail. Black families were disrupted and broken, and millions more became strung out as a result of this substance. And, not to mention, an entire generation of young black men were put behind bars as a result of the discriminatory laws that were put in place for those who sold the substance for financial gain. No need to delve into this subject too deeply, as it is well documented. But, I couldn't not mention an example of the hypocrisy that this nation displays with such normalcy, especially when it pertains to the lives of black and brown people.

A small study from researchers from England and Sweden indicates that listening to music while working could significantly impair creativity. This is interesting, as I'm sure that many would initially think the opposite. I guess the type of work that's being completed may also play a factor.

Another study covered in the paper showed that eating an energizing breakfast and watching less TV leads to a healthier heart. Whoever conducted this study, I feel like they wasted time and resources, as this is common sense. In fact, I'm almost certain that doing these 2 things would lead to nothing but positive results in nearly every category pertaining to the overall human condition. I didn't need a scientific study to be told this.

Lunch was soft shell tacos (meat, beans and cheese), a mix of green beans and peas, white rice, and a small piece of cake. I ate the green beans and peas, some of the rice, and the cake.

Spoke to Elizabeth after lunch today. I speak to her every day though, so there was nothing too special about today's conversation.

Auburn is officially headed to the Final Four of the NCAA tournament. They ousted Kentucky 77-71. This Tigers team is official. However, I do feel for Okeke, one of Auburn's main big men. He tore his ACL in the Sweet 16 game against UNC, and was playing great prior to his injury. I'm sure to not be able to contribute to his team during the remainder of their run is devastating. I tore my ACL the beginning of my senior year during preseason football and was out for the entire football and basketball seasons. So, whenever I see or hear about a great player suffering the same injury, my heart hurts for them. I wish a speedy and fully healed recovery for the young fella.

Played 2 games of Scrabble this evening. I finished 2nd in the first and 3rd in the last.

Dinner was cheeseburger macaroni, a side salad, and yellow cake with white icing. I ate all of the cheeseburger mac, as it was seasoned well again, along with the cake. I wish one day an actual cheeseburger would show up on that tray.

I watched more of the tournament before I turned in for the night. Michigan State beat Duke, 68-67, and will also be heading to the Final Four. Zion Williamson and RJ Barrett both played great games, but RJ missed a key free throw with only seconds left on the clock. Cassius Winston of Michigan State carried his team, making play after play with his craftiness. He definitely showed why he was the Big 10 Player of the Year for the regular season.

I relaxed after watching the game, and eventually took it down to get some rest before work. 1 more day down.

Monday, April 1st, 2019 (For Ermias...)

Hell yea!!! I finally made it to April!! Only 12 more days to go!! Since being in here, in nearly every conversation I've had with my mother, I told her that once I made it to the month of April, I felt that the time would begin to move faster. Although I still have roughly the same amount of time to go as the time I've already served, being in my release month has undoubtedly created a positive psychological effect. I'm no longer climbing uphill, and I feel that I can now actually see the finish line, as opposed to it feeling so far away 2 weeks ago when I arrived.

Work this morning was cool, and as fun as could be given the circumstance. Today was Tran's 52nd birthday. We laughed and cracked jokes on one another about his age and how he thinks I won't look as good as him when I'm that old. He made fun of my bald spot at the top of my head. He joked more about how we both would be coming back to JRDC because we receive free food and don't have to worry about paying any bills. Our relationship has seemingly grown better since we first started working together. He still is an asshole, but appears to be more tolerable than when I first began.

Being in processing following our work shift was somewhat awkward this morning, as I was stripped searched in front of JaNathan, my homeboy who was the CO on duty at the time. At that moment though, I was the inmate and he was the CO, and he was simply doing his job. We got back to our unit around 3:30am. Damn, it felt good to finally cross off a workday for the month of April!

Once back in the unit, Tran usually stays up at least until after he's eaten breakfast. He'll eat while watching TV, while I hop in my bunk to sleep. He always turns it to a DC area news station also, which I appreciate, as it shows more national news and politics. I don't pay too much attention to Baltimore area news when I'm out, being that I work in DC and frequent there more often in general. This morning though, I received some news that I'll never forget.

While laying in my bunk and glancing at the news, a montage of Nipsey Hussle photos came across the screen, with the statement "Rapper Slain" going across the bottom. It then went to commercial. I initially thought that the news was going to mention a rapper in Nipsey's entourage that was killed, because there's no way, I thought, that someone would kill Nipsey. So, when the news came back from commercial, I hopped out of my bed and turned the volume up.

And what I thought couldn't have possibly happened, of course did. They Took Nip Hussle From Us!!! Nah, this can't be. Not Nipsey. Only 33 years young too. According to the news, he was shot and killed outside of his own Marathon Clothing Store in LA. This is another tragic example of prominent rappers who are killed in their own hometowns (Chinx Drugz, Doe B, The Jacka, the list continues). I damn near shed a tear while watching the news. This one is going to sting for a while. For all Nip had done and was continuing to do for his section in LA and beyond, his life was worth so much more for it to be taken so abruptly, and in such heinous fashion.

A lot of people were just recently becoming familiar with Nipsey and his movement, but I had been on him since the summer of 2009, when I first caught wind of his Bullets Ain't Got No Name, Vol. 2 mixtape. Since then, I watched his progression, both in music and in his business ventures. From establishing his own record label All Money In, to opening his Marathon Clothing Store in the Crenshaw district where he was born and raised, to selling his Crenshaw mixtape for $100 as a marketing tactic to attract attention to the product and his brand, to buying back the entire lot (including all of the other stores located therein) where he used to hustle and now where his store is located, to his many other strategic business investments, Nipsey was following the blueprints of ownership and entrepreneurship that forefathers like Hov and Dame, Diddy, Master P, Baby, and J Prince laid out to a T. He also preached this in his music... doing for self, dedicating yourself to a cause, owning what your vision commissioned you to create. He was using the leverage that his platform of music provided to branch off into other ventures such as real estate, technology, food, stem cell research, educational documentaries, and a host of other positive things. He accomplished so much in such a short time, and he was literally just getting started, for he had just begun gaining national notoriety within the past 2-3 years.

But, above all of this, Nip was just a solid nigga all across the board; a man of great integrity, a sharp moral compass, and very difficult not to like and gravitate towards. You could essentially check every category that made him relatable to nearly every member of the "Culture" (African American community) off of the list, for he had it covered across the spectrum. He was from the Crenshaw district of Los Angeles, a famous, yet notorious section where many underprivileged reside, so he could relate to those who came from hostile environments and were forced to live and adapt with the conditions that such areas present. His involvement with the Rolling 60's Crips coming up was well known and documented, so he garnered a high level of respect from those in the streets. He understood the duality of many blacks in America who are of cultural backgrounds other than the United States, as he was of Eritrean heritage. He was tall, handsome, and overflowed with charisma, so women were naturally attracted. Yet, he was extremely intelligent with a keen business sense, thoughtful, very well spoken, and possessed a spirit of service, all of which propelled him into the eyes of the masses.

I'm going on about Nip like I actually knew him, but this is how much I valued what he was doing. I can't believe a sucka really took him out. And if I felt this way about him, then I'm sure that there are plenty of others who share my exact sentiment. I wonder what people's reactions were on the outside when getting the news? I'm sure they received it way earlier than I did, and I'm positive they're in just as much of a state of confusion and disbelief. Folks loved Nip dawg. He was the People's Champ.

There are certain rappers whose interviews I watch simply for inspiration, and Nipsey was one of these individuals, along with others like Hov and 50. Whenever Nipsey spoke in an interview, it was assured that you would leave receiving some useful information, or simply more motivated to do, achieve and attain. People like this, whose deeds provide such inspiration for those around them and beyond, we as a community are supposed to keep uplifted and protected. I'm sure I will hear more about this within the next few days, both from the news as well as from my folks on the outside who had just as much love for Nip as I. None of this is making sense right now. All I know is one of our Kings is no longer with us, and although I'm not out to witness, I'm sure that the entire World is currently in a state of painful disbelief, just as I am. Long Live Nipsey Hussle. The Marathon Will Forever Continue.

Breakfast this morning was French toast (2 pieces), grits, sausage, and chocolate milk. Since I had been up watching the news, I ate this morning. I only had the French toast. I was surprised that it was actually good. I didn't think that they would serve that in here.

I laid back down and rested until lunch. Today, they had bologna and cheese sandwiches, carrots, bread, a side-salad, and pineapples. I didn't eat any of it.

I was told that one of the newer inmates who had just moved into CI last week was fired for being caught sleeping in the kitchen. He was actually moved off of our unit yesterday morning, but I didn't notice because I was sleep. They said that the jail used to write inmate workers up prior to firing them, but they no longer have to perform that initial step.

In today's Capital, I read that there will be Anne Arundel County residents on the show Shark Tank on April 7th. They will be pitching their idea for a cooling system called "Kase Mate", which is able to store up to 30 cans of beer/soda. This is dope. I hope they're able to get one of the investors from the show to put some money behind their idea.

I tried calling my Grandmother twice today but didn't get an answer either time. She may not have been home, or she could've just not stayed on the phone long enough to follow all of the prompts in order to accept my call.

I spoke with Ms. Elizabeth this afternoon. We spoke about Nipsey's death, of course, and how so many people will be impacted as a result. She told me that the shooting actually happened on Sunday afternoon around 3pm. I figured that, due to being in here, I received the news a little later than those on the outside. She said that Nipsey was only making a brief stop at his store, as he was getting some gear for one of his friends who had recently been released from prison. He was there doing a favor for someone else. She also said that, apparently, Nipsey knew the person that shot him, as he was a fellow Crip member from the same area as him. These new facts make the situation even more difficult to process. We also spoke about going out to LA soon to be amongst the love and energy that will undoubtedly be generated because of Nip's death.

Ms. Elizabeth also stated that one of her Instagram comments went viral again, receiving a couple thousand likes. She's witty and, when time permits, will invite the smoke. She'll respond to folks on IG who make remarks that are stupid or not well thought out, especially if it's anything remotely negative about Beyoncé. She also let me know that she had seen results from a juicing cleanse that she began last week. I'm definitely proud of her about that.

This evening's dinner was spaghetti, green beans, bread, and a chocolate chip cookie. I ate most of the spaghetti, the small portion of green beans (although they were cold), and the cookie.

I spoke with my twin cousin Tiffini tonight. I call her that because we were born on the same day and year. I spoke to her about my experience in here thus far, and the things she had going on the outside. She and I are pretty close, so it was good to hear her voice.

Lastly, I spoke with Moms tonight. She told me that my union representative from my job, as well as the hearing officer who had been presiding over my case with the agency, both sent me emails saying that it has been agreed upon that I be reinstated!! God is so good!! I've been on administrative leave from my job since December of 2018 with my livelihood hanging in the balance. Throughout this entire ordeal, I was not as fearful of jail as I was of potentially losing my job. Ultimately, I could handle jail, for I knew it would only be a brief stint. But jail combined with not having a main source of income when I was released was something I greatly feared. For 5 months, this has been my reality, in a state of limbo, waiting to see if I would be reinstated, terminated, or if the case against me would be thrown out altogether. The decision finally came today, and I couldn't have asked for a better result. I had a feeling that I would be reinstated, as my offense, I feel, was nowhere near harsh enough to warrant termination. Also, I've been receiving a paycheck the entire time I've been on administrative leave, and I do not see my agency wasting taxpayer dollars for this long to continue to pay an individual who they intended to fire. But, after not being allowed to report to work for nearly half of a year pending an actual decision, it is only natural for doubt to creep into one's mind.

There was a potential problem with all of this, however. Moms told me that the emails sent to me stated that I was to report back to work on Thursday, April 4th, only 3 days away. Of course, there was no way that this could happen. So, I told my mother to contact my union representative tomorrow and inform her that I would contact her from in here. I wanted to make sure that my union representative would answer my phone call, and not pick up due to seeing a strange number. I would then speak to her about my situation and she could explain to me what my next steps should be. I am hoping that my job will accommodate me due to my current situation and allow my reinstatement to be pushed back until after my release. I mean, it's already been 5 months, so they were clearly taking their time when reaching this decision. Because of this, I'm confident that a couple more weeks will not be that much of an issue.

A lot of the guys in the unit went and got haircuts today. From what I can see, the barber did a good job on cutting them. I already told myself, however, that I was going to let my hair grow while in here. This will definitely be the longest time I've went without getting a cut, but I wanted to purposely let my shit to wolf. Then, the moment that I am released, I'll go to my barber and get a fresh one. I'll use this time to allow my hair to reset and grow back to its original positioning in relation with my hairline. I don't do this enough when I'm out, and I should.

Today was eventful, to say the least. The day started with horrible news, and it ended with the best news I could possibly receive for the time being. All I can do is thank God, as things could've gone in the completely opposite direction for me, and placed my life in even more of a detrimental space as a result. I'm going to lay it down though and see what tomorrow brings. Another day down. R.I.P. Nip.

Tuesday, April 2nd, 2019

Work went smoothly again this morning. On the way to lobby to begin our shift, a CO informed us that a grand jury would be coming to the jail later today, so we should make sure that we do a good job, as if we don't already. Tran and I laughed, joked, and cracked on one another even more this morning. Even after he re-mopped a portion of the floor, we were still finished at a pretty decent time, roughly a little after 3am.

As usual, I didn't even bother getting up to see what breakfast was.

The phones, unexpectedly and unexplainably, went out around 9:30am in the entire jail. They are currently working to discover what caused the problem. They ended up coming back on not too long after though.

In Tuesday's Capital, I read that US Rep. John Sarbanes (D) held a roundtable discussion with various professionals at Anne Arundel Medical Center to discuss gun violence and to generate new ideas about the topic that he could take with him back to DC. Sarbanes is the US Representative for Maryland's 3rd congressional district, which includes the entire state capital of Annapolis. It will be interesting to see what ideas are generated, and if anything productive will actually come from this discussion, since the federal government has been acting in slow motion over the past decade in regards to constructing common sense gun legislation. With this said, it is good to see that at least an effort is being made on behalf of Sarbanes to address one of this nation's most polarizing issues.

I also read that Cambrea May Lynn Sieck, the 18-year-old young woman that was charged as an accessory in the double homicide in Glen Burnie, was released from JRDC Monday afternoon and placed on house arrest. According to the paper, she allegedly assisted the alleged shooter, her boyfriend, by driving him to Mexico following the crime. She is currently 4 months pregnant with her first child, which I assume is the only reason she wasn't held. While on house arrest, she is only allowed to go see her attorney and attend scheduled medical appointments.

Ashling Kitchen and Bar, the new restaurant that opened in Crofton, had their soft opening this past Friday. The official opening of the restaurant is today. Elise Letavish and Saeed Ashrafzadeh, co-owners of the restaurant, first started by opening their catering business to provide food for musical artists backstage at the Lyric Theater in Baltimore in 2016. Elise was also once the tour manager for the late Mac Miller who passed in September. I have to make it a point to check it out once I'm released.

Lunch today was a rice and bean concoction with 1 piece of meat in it, cabbage, cornbread, and a chocolate chip cookie. I ate the cabbage, cornbread, and cookie. The way the main dish was thrown together makes me think that the kitchen is running low on food, and they are trying to stretch out what they have in stock until a new shipment arrives.

Spoke with Moms again this afternoon. She told me that she spoke to my union representative and explained my situation to her. My union rep. stated that she thinks the 2 days that I was asked to initially return (Thursday and Friday, April 4th and 5th) was for some type of orientation or preliminary meetings. She then stated that she thinks I will likely be placed on a 30-day suspension without pay prior to my actual reinstatement. She stated that she would inform her supervisors of my current situation, but it's unlikely that they'd get back with her today.

I was able to speak to my union representative this afternoon as well. I just wanted to touch bases with her personally, as I had already been relayed the necessary information from her through my mother. My union rep stated that Human Resources at my agency wanted to confirm that my release date was April 13th. She stated that she would text any additional information to my mother, and that she would get back to my mother tomorrow with the final word from Human Resources. Everything is sounding positive thus far, and all I can do at this point is to continue to remain positive, hopeful and grateful.

For dinner, we had non seasoned spaghetti style spiral noodles with a big meatball in the middle, another giant meatball on the side, chopped carrots, bread, and yellow cake with a sweet lemon icing. I ate one of the meatballs and most of the noodles.

Played Scrabble again this evening. Finished 3rd. I'm a scrub. I keep getting killed with double and triple word scores.

The Temptations and ATL played one after the other on VH1, and The 5 Heartbeats aired on BET. No better way to cap off an evening in here than with some classic movies. 1 more day in the books.

Wednesday, April 3rd, 2019

All was well at work again today, but things got a little testy between Tran and I once we got back to the unit. I jokingly made a comment to Tran, telling him to clean the crumbs he left on the floor after eating his chips. My tone, I felt, was the same as it always was whenever he and I joke with one another. So, after we both cursed one another back and forth (I was joking, not sure if he was though), he then told me to "suck his dick" numerous times. I'm not sure if he thought that this was a comment that is to be taken lightly, but from what I know, how I was raised and how I conduct myself, this couldn't be further from the truth. It's an unwritten rule amongst men of respect that one man should never tell another man to do this. It's the ultimate insult, above only being spat on. There are usually harsh consequences that follow for the person who made this statement. I've even heard stories as extreme as individuals losing their lives after uttering these words. Not only this, Tran doesn't possess the stature or mindset to think he could seriously say this to another man on the outside and not expect to have his ass thoroughly handed to him.

Under normal circumstances, the results of this interaction between Tran and I would've ended a lot more volatile. In reference to making this statement to another man, the Father of Charlamagne the God, morning radio show host of The Breakfast Club, stated that a man should never say this unless he is prepared to die, or to kill. Not saying that I would've committed an act of violence against him (not saying that I wouldn't have either), but many would argue that speaking this phrase to another man warrants this level of escalation. However, Tran would definitely know, walking away, that this is not a statement that you should feel comfortable saying to another man, jokingly or not. I just replied that I wasn't aware that he liked men to do these things to him. There wasn't much more that I can do in this circumstance without possibly facing a negative consequence. The last thing I wanted to do was get in trouble and potentially lengthen my stay or catch an additional charge. So, I just exercised restraint, walked away and hopped in my bunk, for something a little bigger than my pride was at stake at this point, my freedom.

Breakfast this morning was pancakes, a thick slice of bologna, and milk. I didn't bother getting up to eat any of it.

I received a visit from Ms. Kellie this morning. She informed me that I would now be working in the Administration department of the correctional facility. The previous MIO who worked in this part of the facility had recently been released, so they needed another person to fill this position. I will now be working during the day, from 7:30am to about 12pm, and then again from 1:30pm until about 4pm. Admin is upstairs on the 2nd floor of the facility, and is a bigger area than the downstairs lobby. There's a male and female bathroom, a male and female locker room, both of which are supposed to be swept, mopped and stocked once each shift. I will also be emptying the trash cans at the desks of all of the administrative employees, along with cleaning the windows, vacuuming mats, sweeping and mopping the employee break room area, mopping the hallway 1-2 times per week, and cleaning the equipment in the employee gym. Additionally, I will be called upon, when needed, to pull trash from the large trash bins outside, whenever full, and haul it into the trash compactor. It is seemingly more work, but I am also spending more time out of the unit, which ultimately makes time pass faster. I'm sure that with all I'm being asked to clean, I won't get to each task each day. Overall, I'll have more than enough to keep my busy. I will now get to work alone and at my own pace, without having a co-worker whom I wanted to knock out every other day.

I also found out that I'll be moving to unit C2 right next door. This is because I am now a daytime employee and C2 is considered daytime worker's unit, whereas all of the inmate workers in C1 worked overnight. My visiting hours will stay the same, and even if I work Saturday morning, my visits during this time will always supersede my work hours.

Lunch today was a very lumpy hamburger with potatoes, a side salad, and pineapples. I only ate the potatoes and the pineapples. The way that burger looked was a disgrace to one of America's favorite foods. They should never serve that shit in here again if it's going to look that way.

I spoke with my union rep again today, and she informed me that the official decision has been made concerning my employment with CFSA: I will be reinstated following a 30 workday suspension without pay, which officially began today. They moved the suspension start date to today in order accommodate me and allow me to finish my sentence. The deciding officials ultimately ruled in my favor, agreeing that my offense should've only been reprimanded by way of suspension without pay, and that a request for my termination should've never been proposed. I will be reporting back to work on Wednesday, May 15th. Although I ultimately felt this, and it took them 5 months to come to this conclusion, it still felt amazing to finally receive the official confirmation. God still continues to show me that even in some of my darkest times, He continues to remain on my side. I can't thank Him enough for removing this giant weight off of my shoulders.

I immediately called Elizabeth afterwards and informed her of the news. She pretty much knew what the outcome would be as well, as I had been keeping her abreast of all the prior conversations I had with my union rep, but she, just as I, was also very happy to receive the official word.

I played another game of Scrabble today, and I finally won (first place out of 3 players). About damn time.

For dinner, we had chili, that cake style bread (cornbread style but not the same taste; a little blander), and cake with white icing. I ate some of the chili, all of the cake bread and all of the cake.

In today's Capital, I read that the CVS in Crofton was robbed early Tuesday morning (4/2/19). This is crazy! I go to this CVS all the time. It's literally a 3-minute drive from my crib. I hope all of the victims involved are okay.

I spoke with my main Scrabble buddy today and he explained to me more about the situation that landed him in here. He is currently fighting a Failure to Appear charge from a DUI he received 4 years ago. He stated that the clerk's office repeatedly sent him notices to appear in court, but they were sent to the wrong address. This guy has never lived in any other place than his current address, so the clerk's office has just been sending notices to completely wrong addresses altogether. He has paperwork, which he actually showed me, from the same clerk's office that was sent to 2 completely different addresses, neither of which this man has ever resided! The 2 erroneous addresses were in completely different zip codes. How is a mistake like that even made? He has now been sitting in jail, waiting for his day in court for 3 months, all due to clerical errors from the court. His life has been altered drastically in the process.

This is the part of the justice system that really frustrates me, among many other parts. Although presumed "innocent" until proven guilty, people are still being held in jail, on nonviolent charges, until they have their days in court, or if they have enough money to bail themselves out. If I am considered innocent until convicted, why has my freedom been so quickly and vehemently stripped away, and why must I pay in order to have it returned to me? On top of this, one's regular life can go into complete peril while sitting in jail until their court date. A person can potentially lose all they've worked so hard to attain; jobs, homes, businesses, assets, and complete depletion of funds in an attempt to hire a proper defense, all while awaiting a scheduled court date. And let's not forget to mention the psychological component of all of this, a piece that is not at all discussed enough; being abruptly removed from one's day to day existence and being placed in a real-life hellhole is bound to take a toll on a person's mental stability. Then, if by some miracle they beat all of their charges (the courts stack them up against you so chances of this are slim to none), or are released due to a technicality or for pleading out to a lesser charge, the court does nothing to compensate the individual for potentially derailing their entire life while awaiting court. That individual, in many cases, now has to start from scratch in repairing their life, with absolutely no assistance from the system. This is tragically unfair, and this is one of the many reasons why criminal justice reform is such a hotbed issue in the country today.

My big homie Jaysin came to visit me this evening. I've viewed him as a cousin/big brother ever since he moved to Shady Side when he was 14. He's definitely looked out for me over the years, being there for me at some of my lowest points in my younger adult years. He's always lent a helping hand to me whenever he was able. He's long since been adopted as a member of the family, as have many of my close friends. And not to mention, he's one of the hardest working and most successful friends that I have.

I was definitely glad that one of my dawgs was able to make it to see me. Along with me having such a short stay, all of my homeboys have crazy schedules with families and other obligations, so I wasn't expecting a visit from any of them. But, nevertheless, I was beyond grateful to see at least one of them during my stint here. Jay and I spoke about how everything was going with my situation, as well as some of our future endeavors. He made a great point to me during our conversation. He stated that "we definitely have to start doing a better job of looking out for one another." This is a very real statement. As adults, we all have major responsibilities that pull us in several different directions. Because of this, we at times grow out of touch with our closest friends, the ones who've been there for us and whom we'd call if ever we were in a real jam. His statement was a subtle reminder that we all can do a better job of simply reaching out to our close friends periodically to ensure that our bond remains intact.

Jay also told me that he copped me a ticket to see the Joe Budden Podcast with the rest of the guys. They're doing a live podcast at the Warner Theatre in DC on May 30th. He knew I was a big fan of the podcast, like he is, and he didn't want me to miss a night out with the homies. I couldn't thank him enough for that.

I officially moved out of C1 and into C2 this evening, as I will begin my first day as a daytime employee tomorrow morning. The unit is set up exactly the same as C1, except for everything is on the opposite side. The TV is hung in the front on the left side of the room instead of the right, the phones are on the right instead of the left, and the bathrooms are on the right instead of the left in relation to where my bunk is. I took the first top bunk, so I'm in direct eyesight of the TV once again. Work in admin department starts in the morning. Another 1 down.

C-2

Thursday, April 4th, 2019

Breakfast this morning was a biscuit with sausage gravy, grits, pineapples and chocolate milk. I only ate the pineapples.

Prior to going out for work, Ms. Kellie came past the unit to inform me that my actual release date will be April 16th instead of April 13th. This is definitely unexpected. The last thing an inmate wants to hear is that their release date has been extended. I'm going to try to speak with her again before the day is over, because I suspect that the people in the records department are miscalculating the date I began working and the total number of days I've worked thus far. It's only a 3-day difference, but it feels much longer when it's in reference to prolonging my freedom.

Once I was let out into the lobby to begin my shift, my first task was walking across the street to the visitor's parking lot, accompanied by a CO of course, and changing the trash bags in the cans in the parking lot, the nearby bus stop, and in front of the main entrance. Mr. Somerville, the CO who was in the front lobby when I turned myself in on the 15th, accompanied me across the street. He was the one who looked out for me to ensure that I landed a job during my stay in order to cut my time down. I definitely made sure to thank him for putting in that good word because he certainly didn't have to. During our brief time outside, he and I talked about the job I have on the outside, automobile maintenance for luxury cars, and my plans to begin getting into real estate.

Once back in from gathering the trash outside, I went upstairs and began my duties of cleaning the 2nd floor. I first started by stocking and cleaning each bathroom and locker room, one room at a time. This included re-stocking each room with toilet paper and paper towels, cleaning each toilet, cleaning each mirror, emptying each trash can, and mopping the floors (didn't mop locker room floors). I then went on to clean the windows throughout the main office area. Next, I cleaned the equipment in the gym. After this, I swept, mopped, and emptied the trash in the employee break room. I then vacuumed the rug by the main entrance into the office, and finally, emptied the trash cans sitting by each employee's desk.

Of course, before going back to my cell for lunch, I had to go back to the receiving unit to get strip searched. Since I'll be going out two times each day, I'll now have to get strip searched twice each day. A wonderful addition to the new gig.

I was searched more thoroughly than usual today prior to returning for lunch. It was a CO performing the search who doesn't usually do them, and a more experienced CO was present to ensure that he did it correctly. I'm not sure if this was part of a training, but if so, it made sense. When a training is conducted on any job, the trainer usually shows the trainee the correct and proper way to perform a particular task. Then, as the trainee becomes more seasoned with conducting the activity, he or she develops their own method of performing the task, which is where slight corner-cutting for timeliness usually comes into play.

Normally, when being searched, I just have to squat and cough after taking off my clothes. Today, I had to do this twice, as they didn't realize I had done it once already. Next, I had to spread my cheeks. Then, I had to remove my socks and lift the bottoms of my feet. After that, I had to lift my neck, open my mouth, lift my tongue, and lift my earlobes. After all of this, I still had to wait some more, as the new jump suit that was issued to me to wear consisted of 2 pairs of pants instead of a top and a bottom.

Lunch was pasta salad, ham/turkey smothered in a white sauce (really unsure as to what this shit actually is), chopped carrots, cake-style bread, and yellow cake with powdered sugar on top. The meat and the sauce that it was in looked absolutely disgusting. I only ate the cake-style bread and the dessert cake.

After lunch, I kicked back in the unit until it was time for me to go back out for my second shift. The other guys in C2 work daytime in the kitchen from 10am-7pm, so I essentially have the space to myself all day. This means I can still shower and take a shit in peace. I'm definitely grateful for this.

There was a medical emergency on another unit (D1 I believe), so I wasn't allowed to come out for my second shift until after 2. I also received word that an inmate in the jail (not sure which unit he was in) tried to kill himself today. Hearing shit like this quickly reminds you to not forget that you're still in jail. And, unfortunately, incidents such as this are not at all uncommon in this environment.

I was finished with the 2nd shift around 3:40pm. I swept and mopped both bathrooms and locker rooms on the 2nd floor, emptied all the trash, emptied all the trash in the pre-trial room as well, and vacuumed the rug by the supply room downstairs. I was told by one of the ladies in the pretrial room that their room only gets vacuumed on Fridays.

I had another thorough ass strip search again after my 2nd shift. This time, when issued another orange jump suit to wear, the CO mistakenly gave me 2 right shoes. They said that this is the laundry department's fault, as they put the clothes and shoes together after they've been washed. Having to get searched twice per day now is definitely one of the downsides of working the daytime shift.

I actually found out that my shift times are from 7:30am-11:30am, and 1:30pm-3:30pm. But, in actuality, I can pretty much stop whenever I feel that I've completed the most necessary tasks. There isn't anyone keeping an actual tab on how long I've worked. I just know that in the afternoon, I have to be back downstairs in the lobby by 3:30. The jail does a count of all of the inmates everyday beginning at 4pm, and if I don't make it to the lobby and back to the receiving unit to be searched before the count begins, I'll have to wait for an hour in the lobby until the count is complete.

Dinner this evening was the most tasteless macaroni and cheese I've ever had, a slice of bologna, a side salad (just lettuce though), cake-style bread and a chocolate chip cookie. I ate only 2 bites of the mac and cheese, and the entire piece of bread and cookie.

C2 seems like a livelier tier, which I think is due to the time of their work shift, which is 10am-7:30pm. As soon as they get back in the unit from work, they formulate their teams for Spades, and they play for pushups. They appear to have a closer bond than the guys in C1. I have a sense that most of the guys in here are closer in age, between mid to late 30's, which I think also attributes to the comradery. Everyone has been cool and welcoming so far.

I found out from one of the guys that if you work in this facility prior to being sentenced, then you are paid $2 for each day you work. The payment is placed in your commissary account at the end of each week. You can only get day-for-day once you've already been sentenced.

I spoke to Moms and Elizabeth again today. I told Elizabeth about my mural idea of contacting the artists who did the murals and possibly interviewing them and creating more content for my rap mural Instagram page that I started in January. She thought that it was a good idea. She's always down. She also told me that my mural page gained a few more followers since I've been in. It went from 12 to over 70. I just started it and am still developing the idea, so to see a climb in the number of followers is definitely exciting.

I met a guy in C2 named Eric who's from Calvert County. He said that he has people in Shady Side. I assume he does landscape for work, because he mentioned how he has cut grass down in Avalon Shores, a neighborhood in Shady Side. He also said how he played football for the UYC organization when he was younger. I played football for one year with this organization when I was younger as well. He said he played with brothers Peter and Paul Brown, both of whom are from Shady Side. They actually grew up right down the street from me. They were good friends with my older cousin Vic, and their father, Mr. Danny Brown, was a well-known barber in the neighborhood. Mr. Danny and Peter both have since passed away. Rest in Peace to them.

There was a guy who was from DC that I was in A-1 with who is now in C2. This dude is hilarious. He's in here on theft charges. He's a booster. I think he was caught stealing out of the Burlington Coat Factory in Annapolis.

An inmate I'll simply address as E.V. is in here as well. I never officially met homie until this evening, but I remember hearing and reading his name a lot coming up. In the late 90's (he graduated in 2001), E.V. was the best running back in Anne Arundel County, and arguably the state altogether while in high school. He set many rushing records while at Annapolis, plenty of which I'm sure still stand today. He and I spoke some this evening and he told me about his fall from grace. He told me how he was heavily recruited for football coming out of high school, his top college choices being Michigan and Penn State. But, he got in an altercation where he struck a person so hard, he ended up getting arrested and being charged with attempted murder. Once this happened, all of his recruitment offers dried up, and his life ended up taking some unexpected turns. As the years went by, he worked various jobs, such as driving cabs, line cook at different bars/restaurants, going into the trucking industry and working at the gym. However, he was also getting money out of the street. This, unfortunately snowballed into him having several run-ins with the law for various offenses. He had a couple of opportunities to get back into playing football, but for different reasons, they never panned out. His story was definitely one that was tough to hear. It's always heartbreaking to hear about the paths of people with such talent and promise being derailed due to their circumstances and/or choices they've made.

E.V. is the head cook in the kitchen in here. He mainly mans the grill and also does all of the cooking for the CO's who order sandwiches from the kitchen while on their breaks. He told me that they tried to look out for the previous MIO in their unit since he was here by himself the majority of the day by providing better food to eat. He said that they would continue to try and do the same for me. He said that when the lunch trays are delivered, that I should always take the 3rd tray from the tall stack, as this is the tray on which they sneak the good food for the MIO. E.V. says he's a great cook, and the rest of the guys in C2 vouched for him. I hope he isn't just saying this to get my hopes up, because this definitely has me excited. I'm finally able to eat something good, aside from the bullshit that we're normally served in here. We'll see how everything tastes though. Another I down.

Friday, April 5th, 2019

I didn't bother getting up to see what was for breakfast this morning. It did smell decent though.

I received a lot of compliments while at work this morning from the folks working in the Administration Department. They told me that I had been doing a fantastic job since I started working up there and that everyone has been speaking highly of me. They told me that I am nice, patient, and that their hallways haven't smelled that clean in some time. I was very grateful and appreciative for their kind words. I didn't think I was doing anything too out of the ordinary by performing this custodial work, it's nothing more than basic cleaning to me. Naturally, it made me think of the type of job (or lack thereof) the last MIO did during his time for me to get such high compliments after only working here a couple of days. Nevertheless, it always feels good when your quality work is acknowledged, regardless of your circumstance.

My guy E.V. definitely looked out for me during lunch today. I did as they directed and lifted up the first 2 trays on the tall tray stack and chose the 3rd tray. The CO wasn't paying attention to me while choosing the designated tray, which I noticed they customarily hadn't done, seeing as they automatically assume that all of the trays possess the same thing. This tray had the regular lunch, which was bologna and cheese, white bread, pineapples, a side salad, and chips. But it also had an extra serving of chips, along with 2 fried chicken legs that E.V. whipped up and secretly placed on the tray!! I hadn't had fried chicken since I been here, so this was definitely a blessing. The legs were on point too. I punished them both.

After lunch, while waiting for a CO to come and bring me back out for my 2nd shift, he instead came around and informed me that I had a visitor. This was surprising, because I wasn't expecting a visit today, especially since I knew Moms and Elizabeth were coming on Saturday. Also, it's the middle of the day, and most people I know are, or should be, at work right now.

I walked into the visiting area, and I saw my younger brother Mason on the other side of the glass!! I hadn't told him about me having to come here, so he must've heard the news from our sister, Marlo. Regardless of how he got word, I was super excited to see him, and thankful that I was on his mind enough that he decided to stop past and visit. That really meant a lot to me. He and I chopped it up about how I was doing in here, the tragic passing of Neighborhood Nip, the corporate moves he's been making, the real-estate wholesaling business I just started, and many other things. Each time I talk to him or my younger sister, I always make it a point to tell them how proud I am of them both. They're both young college graduates with great jobs for this point in their young careers. They also both share great vision for their lives as well as the intellect and drive necessary to succeed. Not saying that I didn't possess these things in my mid and late 20's, but I feel that they are definitely at better places in their lives currently than I was at their age. I get so much joy and gratitude witnessing their accomplishments, whether it be from their respective workplaces, to their educational feats, to their travels. I have a front row seat at the show for all of it.

After my visit, I went up to Admin to begin my 2nd shift. While cleaning the female locker room, I briefly spotted one of the black female CO's in the locker rooms preparing to begin her shift. She was reading a book with her headphones in, waving her hand in the air to the beat of the music like she was a rapper. When I returned to my unit once my shift ended, she just so happened to be working our unit the remainder of the evening. Prior to her letting me back into the unit, I joked about spotting her put on her own mini concert earlier. She laughed and stated that she has to do that to get her mind right before coming in here to work her shift. She also said that a lot of her coworkers come to work with attitudes, but that she never takes it that serious. She's been one of my favorite officers since being here. She has a real nice smile, and nice shape for her age too.

Speaking of my sister Marlo, I spoke to her today as well. We had a great convo, like always whenever we speak with one another, even though she thinks she's my mother at times. I love her strength, her work ethic, and how unafraid she is. We talked about the promotion that she finally received on her job, something that was well deserved, and had been long overdue. She also let me know about our cousin Martin recently becoming a father. I'm glad I got to hear her voice, as she shared great news all around.

Dinner was baked chicken, mashed potatoes, carrots, and a cookie. I only ate the chicken and the cookie. The mashed potatoes didn't have any taste.

Spoke to Drew again this evening. I told him about E.V. and I being locked in the same unit, and the unfortunate series of events that happened to him following his historic high school football career. Drew was a freshman at Broadneck High School while E.V. was a senior at Annapolis. He was also already a part of Broadneck's football program, one of the tops in the county, so he definitely remembers E.V.'s record setting years as the Annapolis High School tailback. I'm sure it blew his mind to find out we are now cellmates.

Watched some TV, listened to the guys talk shit while playing Spades, and got in a few laughs with some of the guys before I laid it down. 1 more day down.

Saturday, April 6th, 2019

As usual, didn't get up to see whatever was being served for breakfast.

Received another commissary order this morning. I got 5 bags of BBQ chips, 5 beef and cheese sticks, 5 bags of peanuts, and 5 bags of trail mix.

In today's paper, I read that a gun violence task force would be assembling in Anne Arundel County. Anne Arundel County isn't particularly known for gun violence, as compared to Baltimore County and City. But, coming off of the deadliest year on record in the city of Annapolis (2018), coupled with the mass shooting that occurred at the Capital Gazette headquarters last summer that gained national news coverage, County Executive Stuart Pittman promised to assemble the committee to address this issue.

Bishop Charles Carroll will be the chair of the committee. Mr. Carroll's son, Charles Carroll Jr., or "Swag" as he was known by his peers, was shot and killed in Annapolis back in 2016. He was only 25. I didn't know him personally, but I remember the affect it had on all of his peers, some of with whom we share as mutual friends. It sent a shockwave through the city of Annapolis and left a lot of people devastated. Being that Mr. Carroll knows first-hand the effects that gun violence leaves on a family and community, making him the committee chair seems all the more appropriate.

I also read that the descendants of the Dred Scott vs. Sanford case are calling for reconciliation. Just a brief history lesson, the Dred Scott decision was a historical case in 1857 in which the Supreme Court ruled against enslaved black man Dred Scott, ultimately stating that black folks were not considered citizens.

Now, the descendants of this case have agreed that Confederate monuments should be taken down and moved into museums where folks can further learn about the troubled history of race relations in the America. This decision was endorsed by Dred Scott's great-great- granddaughter Lynne Scott Jackson, along with Charles Taney, great-great-grandnephew of Supreme Court Chief Justice Roger Taney, whose opinion piece about blacks being excluded from American citizenry spearheaded the decision. It's well known that the first step towards change in this nation is the admittance of wrongdoing, followed by making the necessary efforts to correct past wrongdoings. This is only the beginning stages, but I'm definitely interested to see the results of this.

Finally, I read a story about Anthony Weiner, the former U.S. Congressmen for New York who was sent to jail in 2017 for sending sexually explicit material to a minor, having to register as a Level 1 sex offender for the next 20 years.

Work was super cool today. I didn't have to go up to Admin because it was the weekend, and no one was there. I just went across the street to empty the trash cans in the parking lot, emptied the trash cans and vacuumed in the pre-trial room, and vacuumed the 2 rugs in the front lobby. They brought me out to work at 10:20am, and I was done by 11:15am. Couldn't ask for an easier workday.

Lunch didn't go as planned but it could've ended worse than it actually did. The night before, E.V. told me that he would hook me up with a cheeseburger for lunch today. He said it would be wrapped up and placed on the 3rd tray like normal. When the trays came to our unit and it was time for me to get mine, the female CO was watching my every move. They usually aren't this pressed. "They're all the same," she said. As I picked up the 3rd tray and quickly walked back into the unit, she peeped the wrapped burger on my tray and took it away. Damn, I was too blown!! I had my heart set on that burger. And on top of that, there could be some potential backlash that comes from this; like an inmate could lose their job, or they may try to reprimand someone by adding additional time to our sentence for not disclosing who was behind the plan. I doubt that it would go this far, but if so, and if asked anything about it, I'm simply going to say that I didn't know anything extra would be on a tray, but once I saw something that looked better than what was originally on there, I just took it.

So, instead of enjoying a double cheeseburger with lettuce, tomatoes, and barbeque sauce, I was left with the original lunch meal, these weak ass tacos with a chocolate chip cookie. I just ate a beef and cheese stick and bag of chips from my commissary order that came this morning.

I had the cell all to myself for the rest of the day, so I just kicked back, watched TV, and read some more.

While waiting for the 2 NCAA Final Four games to come on later this evening, I watched all of the Friday movies. Each one of them came on the USA network back-to-back.

I swear, I've seen the original Friday at least 1000 times. I could probably recite the entire script backwards if I needed to. But still, even after all this time, I'm still finding little things in the movie that I hadn't noticed before that make the flick even more hysterical. It was just last year that I noticed Craig's girl, Joi, had a nigga laying next to her at the beginning of the movie when she called Craig and questioned him about who he went to the "show" with the night before. I also just recently noticed how Stanley actually tripped and fell after demanding that Smokey and Craig stay off of his grass. This movie came out in '95, and I'm just noticing these small, but funny parts over 20 years after its original release.

This time while watching, I noticed something else. It was in one of the final scenes, when Smokey snuck in the window of Debbie and Felicia's house to steal the $200 that he and Debo took from Stanley's crib earlier that day. Debo began to make a loud snoring sound, and while doing so, inadvertently pushed Felicia out of the bed. I usually always pay attention to that specific part. But this time during this scene, I watched Smokey instead. In those brief seconds, when that sound was made and Felicia was pushed out of the bed, the nigga Smokey stood completely upright like a tree, in fear of moving or making any noise that would potentially wake Debo. It was like he was hiding in plain sight. I laughed too hard once I finally peeped this. It's usually the small things that occur in hood movies with the smaller budgets that turn them into cult classics. Cube definitely possessed the foresight for this early on. Friday is a classic indeed, and Cube is a genius, as proven through this film and many others, his music career, and his countless other successful business ventures.

Dinner this evening was cheeseburger mac, pineapples, and a side salad. I ate about half of the mac, and all of the pineapples. I also ate another bag of my BBQ chips.

We had another movie night tonight. Just as the first time, I went only for the pizza they'd serve while there. I saw one of my homeboys from back in the day in the movie room, my man E Griff. He's related to my homeboy Kerwin, and he used to be with him a lot when we were teenagers. Although he's from Annapolis, he also has family from the Shady Side area. We dapped one another and embraced. I hadn't seen him in a while. It's unfortunate that this is the place where we had to run into one another. I hope whatever legalities he's facing, they all work out in his favor.

The movie shown was The Avengers Ultron, I believe. At least this was a more recent film. Although I knew it was a good movie, I was never that much into the superhero, Marvel, DC (Detective Comics) phenomenon. I didn't grow up reading their comics. I've seen a few of the more popular movies, but not enough to be invested in all of the stories. I ate 2 personal sized pizzas, chips, and 2 chocolate chip cookies while there. The first opportunity the CO gave us to go back to our units, I bounced.

I didn't even get a chance to watch the Final Four games when I got back to the unit. The guys that didn't attend movie night were watching another movie, and they were heavily invested. It actually looked like another Marvel movie. It's all good though, I'll just get the scores from the games once I wake up tomorrow. 1 more day down.

Sunday, April 7th, 2019

Didn't bother getting up again for breakfast this morning. I ate another bag of trail mix I had instead once I finally woke.

I know I said it before, but it's definitely an added blessing and one of the few luxuries I have to be in this unit the majority of the day by myself. I'm able to use the bathroom in peace, just like I did this morning.

The CO working our unit informed me that I probably won't be going out for work today. There isn't much of anything that needs to be done in the lobby. I'll still be getting credit for working though, so I'm not tripping at all.

I read about Revolution Annapolis today in the Capital. It's a congregation that meets at Germantown Elementary School in Annapolis. I read that they recently partnered with a non-profit organization, RIP Michael Debt, to resolve $1.89 million in medical debt in 14 counties in Maryland. Because of this work, there is now an estimated 900 MD families that no longer have overdue medical bills.

RIP Michael Debt is headquartered in New York, and they specialize in buying up and forgiving medical debt, leaving the debtor without any bills or tax burden. This is an awesome story. Incredibly selfless work by both of these organizations.

In The Baltimore Sun, they had a story about a Baltimore documentary called Charm City that's supposed to air on PBS April 22nd. It's directed by Marilyn Ness, and it's going to take a look into the Rose St. community. Everyone's aware of the challenges Baltimore has faced over the past decade. I'll have to remember to check this out once on the outside.

Texas Tech beat Michigan State 61-51, and Virginia beat Auburn 63-62. The NCAA Championship is all set for tomorrow night. I'll definitely be pulling for Virginia. The DMV area has a chance to bring the title back here for the first time since Maryland did it back in 2002.

Lunch was 2 hot dogs, mac and cheese, spicy baked beans, chopped carrots, and a chocolate chip cookie. The mac and cheese was still bland as hell, but it had a tad bit more taste than the last time it was served. I had a few bites of the mac and cheese, a couple of bites of the beans, and the cookie.

I finished The Audacity of Hope today. Great read. Barack proved as an incredible orator during his times as a Senator and later during his presidency, and the same goes for his ability to convey his message on paper. A stark contrast from who we currently have in the White House. His book combined personal life experiences and thoughtful political analysis to produce a brilliant piece of work. What I ultimately took from this book, and from the personal experiences Obama shared therein, is that America is comprised of unique and complex individuals, all of whom having unique and complex experiences and stories that have greatly contributed to shaping their lives. We are not a nation of black and white, but gray. As a result, American politics needs to reflect the complexity of the people that it's attempting to govern. Government must catch up with the majority of this nation, a land of folks who are comprised of more than just one type of school of thought, viewpoint, perspective, and life experience. And above all, despite the struggles we encounter as a country, we must always continue to lead with an unwavering hope for a better tomorrow, for this has ultimately been the type of optimism that has guided this nation since its inception.

Dinner was hamburger over rice and gravy, cabbage, and bread. I ate it all, except for the white bread of course. It was actually cooked well and tasted good. It's a meal that I would've eaten on the outside.

I've literally been in this unit all damn day by myself. I spoke to Moms and Elizabeth today, and got some reading done. I'll be kind of happy once the guys get off of work. I'll at least have some laughs and entertainment.

When the guys came back in this evening, there was an issue between two of them that stemmed from what happened earlier in the kitchen. Erik, the guy who said he knew some folks from Shady Side, didn't like how disrespectfully one of the other inmates spoke to their female supervisor. They were in one another's faces until eventually Erik walked away. The other dude was a young Mexican who looked as if he barely weighed 100lbs. My personal opinion, Erik would've punished the young guy if it actually escalated to that level. I'm glad everything cooled down though.

Carlos, or "Don Pablo" as everyone in the unit calls him, is the oldest guy in C2. I'd guess he's in his early to mid 60's. We're actually bunk buddies, as he sleeps right underneath me. Cool, nice, laid back Mexican guy who hardly speaks any English. He has a gold cap over one of his front teeth too; real old school playa shit. His daughter keeps his commissary full. I guess he was in a giving mood, because he blessed everyone in the unit with snacks from his commissary tonight; chips, mini-Snicker bars, crackers, noodles, etc. Everyone, including myself, thanked him for the love he showed.

Suicide Squad with Will Smith came on the tube to end the night. Another day down. Another day closer.

Monday, April 8th, 2019

Didn't get up for breakfast again, as usual. I could never this early in the morning, unless I'm coming from the club or a long night out. It smelled syrupy though, like pancakes or french toast.

My first shift of work went smooth. I'm still receiving a lot of good compliments from the Administrative employees upstairs. As I was emptying the trash bin in one of the women's offices, she said "You're doing a great job. It's very refreshing." I thanked her and continued on. Regardless of what task you've been assigned to do, and what position you may find yourself in life, it always feels good whenever others recognize you for your good work.

In today's Capital, I read that Michael Busch, longtime MD Speaker of the House, passed away on Sunday after battling pneumonia. He was the longest serving House of Delegates Speaker in Maryland and was a son, and champion, of the city of Annapolis. He attended St. Mary's in Annapolis, the archrival of my alma mater, Severn School. He was loved by many residents throughout the city as well as by fellow legislators. He was known as being a champion for the Chesapeake Bay, Maryland schools, the creative arts, and sports (he was pursued by the NFL as a running back prior to a knee injury). All of the Maryland state flags will be lowered at half-staff today as a result of this great loss.

Lunch today was the infamous "Rottweiler" ball of meat with potatoes, coleslaw, and a coffee cake style bread. I only ate the potatoes. They were good. I also ate some trail mix I had from commissary.

I got pulled out of the unit for my 2nd shift a little early, around 12:45pm. They claimed that I was needed in the lobby, but there was hardly anything that needed to be done. I emptied the trash in the pretrial room as well as the lobby area. Afterwards, I went back upstairs to Admin and did my usual tasks; cleaned those bathrooms and emptied the employees' trash once again. I was done by 2pm, and back in the unit by 2:40.

Talked basketball with one of the CO's while waiting in the lobby after my 2nd shift before being let beck into receiving. He showed me this James Harden commercial on YouTube that he thought was the dopest shit ever. He was a little over excited by it in my opinion. But nonetheless, he was still pretty cool.

Spoke to Elizabeth, Bush, and my dawg Made today. Made said that one of our mutual friends Sierra, or "Boom" as all of her friends call her, wanted to put some money on my books, but she wasn't sure of my account information. I definitely was more than grateful to hear this. I told Made to thank her for me, but to save her money. I'll be home in a week.

There was an issue with the guys' laundry once they got back to the unit from work. Upon receiving their laundry bags, they noticed that some of their belongings were either mixed in with others, or not there altogether. From what I was told, the laundry department washes the clothes of C1 and C2 together, instead of washing each dorm individually. This causes a lot of confusion over where people's belongings end up. This is indeed a problem though, because these inmates pay for all of their clothing (boxers, t-shirts, shorts, sweats, etc., all of these things must be ordered through commissary) and their things are coming up missing.

Virginia brought the NCAA title back to the DMV!! They beat Texas Tech 85-77 in overtime. Great display of strong guard play and overall team basketball by Virginia. Big shots and big plays, one after another. De'Andre Hunter most definitely wrote his ticket to the League with his performance on that big stage tonight. Congrats to the Cavaliers. 1 more day down. 8 more to go.

Tuesday, April 9th, 2019

Didn't waking up for breakfast again this morning. Had to get the CO to grab me another personal hygiene kit so that I could get another toothbrush.

While working this morning in Admin, a CO came to get me to help pull trash to the outside bins.

I had a dope conversation with Scott, one of the guys in this unit with whom I had yet to speak. He just so happened to be in the cell during the time that I'm usually here alone. He was a stocky white guy, probably in his late 30's to early 40's. He said that he actually is in the music business. He runs the social media accounts of EDM (Electronic Dance Music) band Above and Beyond, who are also the owners of a London based EDM music label known as Ajunabeats. They also host a weekly radio show called Group Therapy Radio. We talked about the skewedness and absurdity that is the criminal justice system and how we're actually guilty until proven innocent. We also spoke about our lives outside of here, our jobs, families, his struggles with drugs, and we each shared insights into each other's thought process while being in here. He also revealed his daughter was tragically raped and murdered at age 7. I couldn't imagine the type of anguish and despair that this would cause a person to live with each day. Overall, he definitely seems like a good and sensible guy with a lot of good things to come back to on the outside as long as he's able to stay clean.

Lunch was sloppy joes, green beans, potatoes, and a yellow piece of cake. I ate the potatoes, green beans, cake, and a beef and cheese stick and BBQ chips from my commissary.

After my 2nd shift, I tried to make it back to my unit before they began the daily count. I finished in plenty of time and was back in the lobby by 3pm. I still ended up having to wait another 40 minutes in the receiving unit until after count cleared.

Dinner was "Rottweiler" again, over rice and gravy and a chocolate chip cookie. I ate most of the meal and all of the cookie.

I found out that Scott is also a pretty good Scrabble player. He beat me when we played this evening. Glad I found another person to play with though. We'll go at it some more until it's my time to leave.

One of the guys lost his cool on a phone call with his girl this evening. I'm not sure what was said that had him so pissed, but he was adamant in his frustration. He screamed at her, called her out of her name several times, and afterwards repeatedly slammed the phone while hanging up. He was a younger white guy who seemed immature and, in my opinion, didn't have it all there mentally. Erik came to his aid and tried to talk sensibly to him.

Another day down, and 1 more closer. 7 more to go.

Wednesday, April 10th, 2019

Didn't' wake up for breakfast again this morning.

Prior to going out for work, I swept the front of the unit. For 15 guys living in one place, we keep the area relatively clean. However, we do have to sweep periodically to clean up excess paper, wrappers, trash, etc. that may find itself on the floor over time.

I finished working pretty early today. I was back in the unit before 11am.

In today's paper, I read that no bond would be given for the man who was arrested for planning an attack at the National Harbor. This guy's bond hearing was a mere formality I'm sure, because there's no way a bond would be granted for someone planning a public attack.

Baton Rouge legend Lil Boosie was arrested on guns and drug charges. At least he was no longer on probation when he caught these new charges. I don't know all of the details, but I hope everything works out for him and he keeps his nose clean afterwards. Boosie beat a murder charge a few years back where they were trying to give him the death penalty, so I'm sure he's done with encounters with law enforcement altogether.

There was a big write-up about freshman center Jalen Smith from University of Maryland basketball team, and how he has decided to return for his sophomore season. I remember watching him in high school last season while attending Mt. St. Joseph's in Baltimore. They came down to play Severn during a game over winter break. He dominated. I loved the statements that his mom made to the paper about him actually liking school, being a smart kid who happened to play basketball, and him not having to rush to be an adult. These were extremely important words.

Also, Annapolis mayor Buckley was questioned by the City Council about using a law firm to whom he has close ties with to file the $400 million lawsuit against opioid producers. While the Mayor felt that a local firm would be most fitting to use, some of the City Council members disagreed with Buckley using a firm that has already represented him in other personal matters.

For lunch, we were served bologna and cheese sandwiches, pasta salad, chopped carrots, and a chocolate chip cookie. I had the cookie and more trail mix from commissary.

I didn't even go out for my 2nd shift this afternoon. The CO said that Admin didn't call for me, but Admin never calls for me. I just know to go back there in the afternoon. I think there may be some confusion among the CO's who work our unit as to what I do and where I work. Regardless, I'm not trippin' at all. I still get credited for working, and now I have the rest of the day to kick back.

On ESPN, I saw that Magic Johnson is stepping down as the Laker President of Basketball Operations. This is very interesting, as it could potentially bring great change to the dynamics of that organization. Magic was a big reason for King James coming there, and a big reason why the Lake Show has still been able to sell tickets over the past few losing seasons post Kobe Bryant. I'm sure that I'll hear a lot more about this story as it further develops over the next few days.

Dinner this evening was some watery ass spaghetti that wasn't seasoned at all, green beans and chopped carrots, cake style bread, and a chocolate chip cookie. I ate the veggies, bread, and the cookie. Scott gave me an extra bread that he didn't want, so I ate that too.

Moms and Elizabeth visited me today. It was awesome seeing them both. We had our normal discussions of how things were in here for me on the day to day, how their days had been and what they had been up to on the outside, and the anticipation of my release.

Our unit had a shake-down while I was on my visit. I'm not sure the reason behind this one, or if it was completely random. When I arrived back to the unit, all of our lights were on and the inmates were going through their belongings that had been ransacked. Some of their things were misplaced in the process. All of the guys were understandably angry behind this. Thankfully, none of my things were misplaced or taken. I don't have much to go through anyway.

2 guys left the unit today. One of them was the white guy Scott. Before he left, he let me get the book that he completed while he was in here, Autobiography of Nelson Mandela. He said that it was one of the greatest works he's read, and the inconveniences that inmates face in here pale in comparison to the amount of hardship Madiba encountered during his time behind bars. I know the broad story of South African apartheid and the lifelong fight of Mandela to end this injustice, but I've yet to read his words for myself. It's super long, so there's no way I'll finish it between now and the 16th, but I'm definitely excited to read what I can for the remainder of my time.

In less than a week, that'll be me getting to leave. The 16th definitely can't come fast enough. Another day down. Only 6 more to go.

Thursday, April 11th, 2019

Didn't wake up to see what was for breakfast.

Work was busier than usual this morning. Anne Arundel County Executive Steuart Pittman and members of his team were visiting Admin and meeting with some of their staff. Because of this, there were a couple of extra tasks I was instructed to perform on top of my daily cleaning duties. I had to make 2 trips to the big recycling bin on the outside of the facility to dump the boxes that had been overflowing in the Admin break room for the past week. Additionally, I had to thoroughly clean the table in the conference room and assist with the refreshment tray layout. I was sent to the kitchen to retrieve a large enough bowl to put ice in. I saw the guys that I'm in C2 with behind the grill, cooking and prepping food to take orders for the staff and CO's who come in on their lunch breaks. Damn, I'd give almost anything to have a burger or cheesesteak on my tray for lunch. Wishful thinking though.

After my 1st shift, while waiting in receiving to go back to the unit after being searched, I heard a voice from the receiving bullpen loudly say, "Hey Shady Side!" I figured he was referring to me, so I turned to the right to see who it may be. It was 1 of my uncle's close friends from high school. They were once teammates, hooping alongside one another for Southern High School back in the day. He had known me since I was a youngin' being around my grandmother's house, and was very familiar with a lot of my other family members. He said, "Yea, you're Therla's son." "Yea, that's me, what's happening," I replied. It's my understanding that most folks in our small town know that he has had more than his fair share of run-ins with the law over the years, most of which I assume were for drugs. He told me that the police pulled him over last night by the Chic-Fil-A in Annapolis and found cocaine and other paraphernalia on his person. He went on to talk about how the police impounded his truck, but he still has yet to pay it off.

He then began talking about the tragic case of Kirk Matthews, or "Sidewinder" as he's known in Shady Side. Sidewinder was sentenced to 80 years earlier this year after being convicted of a double homicide shooting that occurred on Scott Town Lane in Shady Side during the summer of 2017. Scott Town Lane has maintained a reputation over decades as being an area known for drug activity in Shady Side. And, from the stories I've heard and what was presented in the paper, the incident may have been drug related.

Shady Side is such a small town. So, whenever something unfortunate happens to a person or family of this community, the news travels quickly. And, being that all of the black folks who are from here either know, grew up with, or are related to one another, it has an affect on us all. My uncle's friend spoke about how much he would miss Sidewinder, as they've known each other their entire lives. He also expressed concern for Sidewinder's safety while in a state penitentiary since he isn't affiliated with any gangs who he could turn to for protection while inside. He stated that, because of this, Sidewinder should either join a basketball team or immerse himself in the church in order to avoid unwanted confrontations. These must be the groups who receive passes in the state jails. Unc's friend informed me that he's done time in many of the state facilities (Jessup, Hagerstown, Eastern Shore), so he's aware of certain protocols.

Unc's homeboy even told me the name of the person from the neighborhood who allegedly snitched on Sidewinder. I swear, he just kept talking without any provoking from me at all. He said that the Anne Arundel County Police "promised" a hefty reward sum for anyone who came forward with information about the shooter. He said the person who ended up coming forward didn't even receive the money that he expected once he provided the info. He said that there were some other individuals, all known frequenters of Scott Town Lane, who people may have suspected of telling due to their circumstances and wanting to collect the reward money. But either way, according to him, no money was ever given by the police in exchange for information. I'm not sure how true any of this shit is, but it definitely made for an entertaining story while I was waiting to leave receiving. I hope everything works out for the big homie in the meantime, and Sidewinder too. Terrible story all around. I made it back to C2 just as the lunch trays were arriving.

Instead of that cheesesteak I was wishing for in the kitchen earlier, my lunch was a hot dog (not sure whether beef or pork), chopped carrots, rice, bread, and a chocolate chip cookie. I ate a few scoops of the rice, my trail mix from commissary, and the cookie.

In today's Capital, I read that the skeletal remains discovered along the shoreline in Shady Side in late 2017 were of an Annapolis woman by the name of Megan Tilman. Megan was said to have been developmentally disabled. It's still unsure as to what was her actual cause of death. I hope the family of this woman receives the answers they need in order to gain closure. This is definitely a sad case.

An Anne Arundel County Sheriff employee was sentenced to a year and a day in federal prison for leaking sealed indictment information to the Annapolis guys who were convicted and sentenced last month for their involvement in drug trafficking throughout Annapolis and surrounding areas. She had essentially been telling them the details of their investigation and when their indictments would be coming. This case, and all of its details, damn near plays out like a movie, or a documentary one may end up coming across about a crew's rise to fame in the streets and their eventual downfall. I've always loved a good street story, but the outcomes are hardly ever positive for those involved. This shit seems no different.

Key School, a prestigious small private school in Annapolis, will be providing support and creating a therapy fund for alumni of the school who were victims of sexual abuse. Earlier this year, the school released a report uncovering decades of sexual misconduct within the school that went unaddressed. This is happening following a bill that failed to pass through the MD General Assembly that would've allowed child sexual abuse survivors more time to file lawsuits. This is a crazy ass story, one in which I had absolutely no idea. Key School did a great job of keeping this horrific news swept under the rug for so long, but overall, this is great news for the victims of the past traumas that occurred at this school. I hope that the treatment to which they now have access provides them with a source of healing and comfort.

I made it back into C2 right before they began count this afternoon. I had to pull trash out of the large bins again this afternoon and toss them into the compactor. This is probably the busiest day I've had since I began working in here. Even then, the work isn't as demanding as the guys working in the kitchen 9 hours a day, so I'm not complaining.

I was able to catch a good portion of Nipsey Hussle's funeral that was aired live on BET (#BETRemembersNipsey). I came in during Blacc Sam's speech (Nipsey's older brother). For just losing his brother in such a terrible fashion, Sam was incredibly calm and poised. He spoke about the plans he and Nip always had of ownership and being businessmen, the struggles they encountered on their journey, and the perseverance they displayed in order to push towards their goals.

"Boogie" (Lauren London) gave an amazing speech also. She shared an intimate text message with those in attendance that she sent to Nip 1 morning while he was sleeping so that when he woke up, he could read it. She said that she loved to watch him sleep. She conveyed some of the qualities that explained Nip's intelligence and sharpness. She informed the audience that "He (Nip) researched everything, completely self-taught. He played audiobooks before he went to sleep."

She wrapped up her speech by leaving the audience with some motivational words from Nip himself: "The game is going to test you. Never fold. Stay 10 toes down. It's not on you, it's in you. And what's in you, they can NOT take away."

Former President (but forever President) Obama even wrote a letter honoring Nipsey, which was read by Nip's family. Barack informed everyone that he initially learned of Nipsey through his children and, from there, familiarized himself more to Nip's transformation, and the community work he did in order to uplift his district and the residing therein. To have a person of this magnitude and importance take the time to recognize the contributions you made in such a short time is truly incredible.

Along with close family, other celebrity guest speakers included Y.G., Snoop

Dogg, and a performance by the iconic Stevie Wonder.

Pastor Shep Crawford also gave a great ending speech to wrap up the funeral. He provided gems for everyone to take away and apply, all the while ensuring that it all tied back to Nipsey's Victory Lap/Marathon brands. He said, "The race is not given to the swift or the strong, but the one who endures until the end." Exactly. Long Live Neighborhood Nip!!

Dinner was the good ol' "Rottweiler" meat over rice and gravy, cabbage, bread, and honeydew melon. Nothing was seasoned well, so I only ate a few bites, and ate all of the melon. Other than the fruit, this was the same shit we had on Tuesday, just not as well seasoned.

Another inmate left today. Only 5 more days now until I'll be the one being released. 1 more day down. 1 more closer.

Friday, April 12th, 2019

Slept through breakfast again. Didn't bother waking up.

I began my work shift this morning outside. I was instructed to sweep in between the cracks of the outside main entrance to remove old dirt and cigarette butts that compiled in the area over time. I'd say I did a good job, as there is a noticeable difference to the front entrance than to when I started initially. Performing this task gave me visions of my grandmother, as it reminded me of her sweeping the walkway right outside of the front door early summer mornings, right after the sun rose.

That image of my grandmother always makes me laugh though, because it reminds me of something I heard a comedian once say about older people, and the statement couldn't hold more truth, especially in regards to my NaNa. I can't remember which comedian specifically (I feel like it was Steve Harvey), but he essentially made the observation of how older black folks are up at the crack of dawn and begin working as soon as they rise, usually performing random non-pertinent tasks, because they aren't too sure how much time they have left. Not saying that death is coming to anyone anytime soon, but my grandmother sweeping in the morning is a perfect example of this comedian's commentary.

Around 10am, I was pulled from working in Admin. I was told that one of the CO's was going to the armory where all of the weapons are stored. And, as a safety precaution, I was sent back to my unit early. My morning shift was ended early. No problem at all to me.

Lunch was hot dogs, beans potatoes, coleslaw, and cake with icing. I only ate the potatoes and the cake.

I wrapped up my second shift and made it back to the lobby by 2:30pm this afternoon. The CO yesterday told me that if I wanted to make sure that I didn't get stuck waiting in the lobby until after count cleared, then try to be back by this time. I adhered to his suggestion. I emptied the trash and vacuumed in the pre-trial room, cleaned the upstairs bathroom, and emptied the Admin employee trash. I was back in the unit by 2:45pm, way before count began.

In the Capital for today, I read about Rida Alvi from Annapolis High School being the newly elected student member of the Anne Arundel Board of Education. I found it interesting to learn that the Anne Arundel County school board is the only local body in the nation to grant its student members full voting rights.

I cooked some noodles for the first time since being in here. "Don Pablo" gave me a few packets of noodles from his commissary. Being that we can't boil water in here, the only way to cook the noodles is to sit them in a bowl, pour hot water from the sink or shower into the bowl until the noodles are completely covered, put the top on the bowl, and let them sit to allow the water to cook through. Afterwards, drain the excess water (which is now not hot at all) and add whatever seasoning packets you have. They weren't too bad, considering the circumstances under which they were being prepared.

Dinner this evening was roasted chicken, mashed potatoes and gravy, chopped carrots, cake bread, and cake with icing. The chicken tasted good. It was crispy and the skin was seasoned well, so I definitely ate all of it. They dropped the ball on the potatoes though. And those chopped carrots they serve us come from straight out of a can, with more water than actual carrot, so I never eat them. I only ate the chicken, the bread, and the cake.

Had another good convo with E.V. tonight about his situation and the reason for him being behind bars. He expressed great concern for his son, and how since he's been locked up, his son doesn't have any fixed place to stay. He suspects that he may be staying with a girl in the Crofton area, but is not certain. He fears that his son may make the wrong decisions in his absence and wants nothing more than to get out and get back to him. Because of this, he decided to write a letter to the judge presiding over his case expressing the severity of the situation regarding his son. He allowed me to read it and asked my opinion. Despite some of the spelling errors, I thought that it was heartfelt overall. I encouraged him to send it to the judge as soon as possible, as it can only help his current situation.

While talking to E.V. I caught the younger inmate (same one who cursed out his girl over the phone) performing a Power Ranger/Kung Fu style workout routine in the front of the unit. Super unorthodox, awkward ass movements. My man was really into it too, breaking a sweat and all types of extra shit. This was, by far, the funniest shit I've seen since I been in here. I laughed uncontrollably.

Another one of the guys left today. That's 4 since Wednesday. Dudes are bouncin' left and right.

Shit did get a little hectic at the end of the night. One of the guys suspected that the inmate who was released earlier today stole a couple of bags of coffee out of his bin before he left. Scott, who was released a few days ago, mentioned to me that this guy may be schizophrenic, so as I watched him carry on over this coffee, it began to make sense. This guy spent a good portion of the night walking frantically around the unit, playing out different scenarios as to who in here could've possibly taken his stuff. After his final phone call, while the rest of us were laying down for the night, he stood on top of the table nearest the phone and yelled, "Whoever in here took my shit, whenever I find out I'm going to crack your fucking skull wide the fuck open!! I don't give a fuck who it is!"

Coffee is a big thing in jail, but I highly doubt anyone in here took any of his. But nonetheless, no one in the unit responded. They just let him vent, and eventually he laid down too. Thank God I only have 4 more days of this shit. Another day down.

Saturday, April 13th, 2019

Snoozed through breakfast as usual. It's Saturday, so I doubt I'll be going out to do any work today. If so, it won't be much.

I read a few dope stories in Saturday's Capital:

The All Anne Arundel County basketball team was named in the paper. My homeboy Kerwin's nephew, Daevone Johnson, was named the Anne Arundel County Player of the Year. Old Mill has run county basketball over the past few years, and Kerwin was one of the top players in the county when he was in high school, so I'm not too surprised. Daevone was the all-around utility man for Old Mill. Whether it was a bucket, assist, steal, block, rebound, he always came through with a big play for his team whenever one was needed.

AJ Burch from Severn School, my alma mater, was also selected. It said he averaged over 18ppg his senior year and scored over 1,000 points for his high school career.

High Point University, the D1 school that my cousin Curtis is hooping for currently, will have another player from Anne Arundel County joining their squad for the upcoming season. Khalil Williams from Indian Creek, a small private high school right outside of Annapolis in Crownsville, was recruited to come and join the Panthers. He also had a great high school career, scoring 900 points in 3 seasons with Indian Creek, averaging 18ppg his senior year, and making the All-County squad. I'll definitely be going to check out more High Point games this upcoming season.

Disney unveiled their plan for their upcoming streaming service, Disney Plus. With Apple and now Disney releasing their own streaming platforms, there's going to be a lot of pressure placed on Netflix, Hulu, etc. Shit, in 10-15 years, cable will be gone entirely due to the plethora of streaming services of which one can choose. It's crazy to think how much technology, and the way we consume information, has changed so drastically over time.

Opioid use and overdoses have been an extreme concern in the county over the past 5 years. On a positive note, the paper revealed that opioid overdoses have decreased by nearly 25% in the county since this time last year. So far this year, there have been 234 total OD's, and 34 fatal OD's, when compared to last year at this same time, there were 310 total OD's, and 59 fatal.

The students at Georgetown University in D.C. have voted to establish a fund to benefit descendants of the 278 slaves the institution sold back in 1838 to help pay off the debt it had at the time. The students have voted in favor of raising their tuition $27.20 per semester in order to do this. If approved by the university, this will be one of the 1st reparation funds established by a major U.S. institution. There's been much empty rhetoric lately from politicians about their plans (or lack thereof) to provide a form of reparations to African Descendants of Slaves in this nation, yet there has been no plan presented by any of them that seriously outlines actionable items. A college institution has decided to lead the charge of this campaign, providing a practical example, although on a smaller scale, of how this could be accomplished, and not just used as a talking point. I couldn't be more excited to hear about it.

Harvard grad and expert test taker Mark Riddell plead guilty to fraud, money laundering, and conspiracy in the college admissions scandal that has taken the country by storm most recently. They said that this dude was so smart, you could actually pick what test score you wanted on the SAT or ACT exams, and he could get it for you. That's a different level of brilliance. He fixed the test of actress Felicity Huffman's daughter, as he was paid $15,000 by Huffman to correct her daughter's answers once she completed the test. It's crazy to think of the things to which privilege can grant you access.

The NBA Playoffs start today!! Games will be on all day on ESPN, 2:30-10:30pm. What better way to spend a Saturday afternoon than to watch some playoff bump, minus the steel bars and orange jump suit?!

Had my last visit from Moms and Elizabeth today. They both said that everyone working out in the lobby spoke highly of me. The white female receptionist said that they wish they could keep me. I know that was a compliment that spoke to my work ethic and attitude, but that's definitely not happening. The white CO who I've talked basketball with told my Moms that if I ever needed help finding a job, or anything along those lines, to let him know. He also told her that whatever I ended up doing in life, I'd be successful at it.

This facility receives dozens of visitors per week. So, for these people, who don't know me as anything other than an inmate, to speak so positively about me to my people, it definitely means something. Circumstances, such as my current situation, are merely temporary. One day a person could be broke, the next they could be rich beyond measure. But, it's the character and a person's overall nature that will always pierce through whatever circumstance one may find his or herself. This is what people truly remember about a person. Because of this, I'll always feel good when others notice my good character and I'm able to leave them with a positive impression. That feeling never gets old.

Today's lunch was macaroni noodles in a spaghetti style meat sauce, cabbage, bread, and cake with icing. The cabbage was seasoned well, so I ate all of that, as well as the cake.

My final commissary order came in today. I ordered a pair of flip flops. I'm only here a few more days, but I'll be putting these to use on the outside as well. They resemble Adidas, so I figure I could rock them with my Adidas track pants when I'm out and about running errands. I also ordered another 2 bags of trail mix, and another pair of boxers, which didn't even come in. This money is supposed to go back to my commissary account, but at this point, I could care less whether or not it makes it back there. I'm rolling out in 3 days.

I did end up being pulled from the unit to empty the trash bins and the recycling outside. I was brought out around 1:35pm and was back in by 2:05. It rained earlier this morning, but it eventually cleared, and ended up being nice by the time I was brought outside.

Dinner was bologna, beans, broccoli, cornbread, and honeydew melon. I ate my trail mix instead, along with the cornbread and the melon.

I saw a damn salamander crawling around in the unit while I was on the phone. I didn't say anything to any of the guys when they came back in from work though. I figured it be better if they didn't know, or they realized it on their own if it reappeared. I didn't want to cause any unnecessary commotion.

The first games of the first round NBA Playoffs were all entertaining. The

Nets beat Philly 111-102. Orlando beat Toronto 104-101. DJ Augustin had a big game and hit a big shot towards the end to bring home the W for the Magic. Golden State beat the Clippers 121-104. Steph Curry passed Jesus Shuttlesworth as the all-time playoff leader in made 3-point field goals. More Game 1's tomorrow. Nothing better than the NBA Playoffs. Only 3 more days until I'll be able to watch them in my own crib.

Sunday April 14th, 2019

Slept for breakfast.

I was brought out to the lobby around 7:30am to go across the street to empty the trash bins in the parking lot. I was back in the unit by 8:05am. While in the lobby waiting to go outside, the receptionist on duty said to me, "I don't know how you do it, but you always have the sweetest demeanor." I thanked her and replied by saying that there wasn't any sense in walking around angry.

Before being brought out this morning, the movie Ocean's 11 was just coming on. I always watch the Ocean's movies whenever they're on TV. George Clooney is one of my favorite actors, and he's by far one of the coolest guys to be on the big screen. In the beginning of the movie, it shows Clooney's character, Danny Ocean, being released from jail. Then, he and a team of smooth criminals go on to devise an intricate scheme to rob a casino of millions. They do just that and get away without being caught. The Ocean's movie series is one where the audience roots for the "bad guys" to win, and they feel good doing so because of how they go about their criminal acts; smoothly, with style, tastefulness, discretion, and they remain fly while doing it. It's like watching the Rat Pack, but for crooks. While watching, I found myself channeling my inner Danny Ocean. When Danny got out of jail, he essentially devised a scheme to collect a major bag. And he did it. I thought to myself, "This is exactly what I plan to do once I leave." Only difference is I'll be taking the legal route to get mine.

E.V. told me that he gave the inmate who bugged out last night a packet of his coffee to ease any tension that could potentially be had in the unit over his anger of someone allegedly taking his things. Small gestures go a long way, even in jail.

Lunch today was a bologna sandwich. No cheese though, just the meat and 2 pieces of bread. Also, a side salad, and a chocolate chip cookie. I just ate some trail mix, along with the cookie.

In the Baltimore Sun, I read that Morehouse, the historic male African American college in Atlanta, Georgia, will begin admitting transgender men into its institution in 2020. However, students who identify as women but were born men cannot enroll. This sounds a little confusing to me, and this is probably because I'm not super educated in the topic. I'll need to do more research on the transgender community because I know that its intricacies extend way beyond my surface understanding.

I was pulled from the unit again around 1:30pm to pull the trash and recycling outside. I was back by 2pm.

This evening's dinner was ground beef over some watery rice, a side salad, cake bread and banana-nut style bread. I used a hot & spicy seasoning from the noodle pack I had on the rice and meat. Shout out to Dread for schooling me to this a few weeks ago. I was then able to eat the dish, along with the bread.

2nd day of game 1's for the 1st round of the NBA Playoffs!!
Final Scores:
Boston over Indiana, 84-74

Portland over OKC, 104-99
Bucks over Pistons, 121-86
Rockets over Jazz, 122-90

Tiger Woods won his 5th Masters tournament today!! Definitely happy to see this. Tiger has dealt with his own personal struggles over the last decade. I'm glad to see him reach the top of the mountain once again.

I spoke to a Mexican guy who just moved into C2. I remember being in A1 with him when I first got in. I'd say he's in his late 40's or early 50's. He told me that he was in on a DUI too. He came in on March 16th, but he's being held without bail until his court date in June!! The court is making him sit in jail 3 months to await sentencing for a DUI charge. He'll be in jail awaiting his sentence longer than my actual sentence altogether. And I believe this is his 2nd DUI offense, as it is mine. This is beyond excessive to me. He said that he thinks he's being held because the courts may think that he's in the country illegally. Not to mention, he has a house in Bowie with a mortgage of over $2k that still must be paid, along with a wife and children that he was supporting with his income. It's the real-life shit that a person suffers when they're being forced to sit and await trial or sentencing, particularly for a non-violent charge. A raw deal dealt indeed.

Around 8:30pm I was called out for a 3rd time. This is unusual, as I've never been called out at night. Once in the lobby, I couldn't believe the task I had been instructed to perform. Apparently, a woman who came to visit an inmate had a miscarriage right in the damn visiting room! There was a pool of blood lying right in the middle of the visiting room. What was even crazier was that folks were still in there, talking on the phones through the glass to their incarcerated loved ones as if this big puddle of blood wasn't here. I would've assumed that under these circumstances, a CO, lobby receptionist, or someone would've at least cleared the area until this mess was cleaned. There are so many questions I have. I'm not sure of the circumstances entirely, as I wasn't there when it happened, but a miscarriage is, in my opinion, no way something that a county jail is equipped to handle. And I know that I'm technically a custodian that works for the jail, but damn. I didn't sign up for this type of shit.

Unfortunately, the responsibility of cleaning the area still fell on me. I put on gloves and proceeded to spray the entire area down with bleach. Then I mopped the entire visiting area. I also disinfected the visiting booth in which the woman sat, including the glass, steel stool, and the phone. Afterwards, I discarded the mop head into a bio-hazardous bag, then put that into its own trash bag.

I didn't even get a chance to watch the rest of the playoff games because of this emergency cleanup, although I got the scores. The rest of the guys started watching another movie when I left. Once I got back in, I just laid down and went to sleep, still trying to fully process what just happened in the visiting area. A woman really had a miscarriage out there. This was definitely one of the crazier experiences of which I've ever been apart. Thankfully, I only have 2 more days left in this bitch.

Monday, April 15th, 2019

Breakfast smelled syrupy again, like it was pancakes. Still didn't bother getting out of bed to get any of it though.

Since I'm about to be out of here, the jail had to find another inmate to replace me as the daytime MIO. He's a white guy named Nash, probably in his mid to late 50's. He was short and tatted. Cool, laid back guy overall. I can tell from his walk, talk, and overall vibe that he's spent a lot of his time around Brothers. He was well known in the jail, as he had been in and out for some time, and even worked as a MIO during a prior bid. The CO's as well as the supervisor of Admin knew him by name. He's a pretty good worker too. I showed him where all of the supplies were kept and showed him my daily routine of cleaning the Admin Department, as well as the order in which I cleaned everything. He was receptive to everything, but I also let him know that if he had his own methods or prefers to do things in another order, then feel free to do so. Since there were 2 of us cleaning this morning, we were able to finish earlier than usual, knocking everything out by 10am.

While waiting in the lobby to go back to receiving, Nash and I were talking with the CO, the same one who I had convo's with about basketball whenever he's on duty. Both he and Nash know one another from Nash's previous stays. I was talking to them about how prior to working during the day, I was a nighttime MIO working with Tran. I explained to them how much of an asshole he was. When I told them that Tran told me that this would be his first and last time here, they both laughed. After I described him, Nash stated that he remembers being locked up with him before. The CO then confirmed that Tran has definitely done time here. He said that they have multiple booking photos of Tran, at least 12 to be exact!! I couldn't help but to laugh at that. Tran had no reason to lie to me about this, especially since I never even asked him about how many times he's been locked up. Shit, I could care less. I sure hope this was his last time though, because I'm sure that the CO's in here are tired of dealing with him and his crazy ass antics each time he returns.

I told the CO that tomorrow I'd be getting released. He shook my hand and told me that it was a pleasure to meet and speak with me. He then said to me what he told my Moms a few days ago, that I'd be successful in whatever I decided to do. I thanked him for his kind words, then went back in to receiving.

Lunch today was hot dogs with bread, cabbage, potatoes, and cake with powdered sugar. The cabbage and potatoes were seasoned well, so I put those down. They both were good. I also ate the cake.

The 2nd shift went by quickly as well. Nash and I knocked out the bathrooms, trash, as well as the trash outside in an hour. We were done by 2pm.

Dinner was spaghetti, green beans, bread and cake with powdered sugar. I ate half of the spaghetti, all of those unseasoned ass green beans, and the cake.

I didn't watch any of the game 2 playoff games tonight. The guys were watching a movie again, so I just kicked back the rest of the evening. I'll get the scores and see the highlights from them tomorrow, which also happens to be my last day in this bitch!! Tonight will be my last night spent in JRDC. This time tomorrow, I'll be in my own crib, eating good, surrounded by my loved ones, and enjoying my freedom. I'm more than ready.

Tuesday, April 16th, 2019

Slept through breakfast again this morning.

Waking up this morning felt different. I knew that by the end of the day, I'd be a free man. No more orange jump suits, cleaning other people's bathrooms or emptying their trash, strip searches, shake downs, sharing my living quarters with other grown men, uncomfortable ass beds, disgusting food, and overall being viewed as less than.

In order to be released today, I still had to work. So, Nash and I went up to Admin and handled our business. We were done with all of the cleaning upstairs by 9am. Since we were done so early, the facilities supervisor asked that we go outside in front of the main entrance and pull some weeds out of the mulch beds.

Prior to going outside, the facilities supervisor, a middle-aged black woman, asked me, "So what's a nice young man like you doing in a place like this?" She was cool, and always treated me respectfully during my time cleaning in that area.

I replied that I simply made a mistake and I was here to be held accountable for my actions. She acknowledged my answer, and replied by saying that everyone, even herself, is essentially one mistake, slip-up or negative encounter away from being here. She then wished me good luck, encouraged me to stay out, and to continue doing good things on the outside. I assured her that I would.

While outside pulling weeds, I informed Nash about how I had to clean the visitor's room after the miscarriage a couple of nights ago, and all the blood that was present. He told me that I shouldn't have been instructed to do that. He informed me that in prison (not jail), any inmates who have jobs cleaning blood spills are required to receive various shots prior to attaining that position. Only inmates with long bids are eligible to acquire such positions in there. I had no idea about any of this. I wish I would've known, because I definitely would've said something prior to them telling me to clean that blood-filled area. But what's done is done now.

After work and being searched, the CO said that I'd be called between 12:30 and 1pm, no later than 1:30, to be released. I was happy as hell to hear these words, but I wasn't expecting to be released so early. I was thinking that I wouldn't be let out until sometime in the evening after the count cleared. It's all good though. Shit, I'll just call an Uber or Lyft to get home if no one can come to scoop me, since it's right in the middle of the day. I called Elizabeth and Moms to let them know the details and that I'd find my own way home. I told them just to meet me at the crib as soon as they could this afternoon.

I then began getting myself together by going through all of the shit in my blue bin. I threw away some things I didn't need and put the things I would be taking with me in my netted laundry bag. I left a note on E.V.'s bed telling him good luck with his situation as well as my number.

Took my last shower and put on a pair of fresh boxers I had been saving for the last day. I wanted to make sure that I no longer had the stench of captivity on me prior to being released. It was one of the best showers I've taken. I'll feel back to my regular self once I go and get a haircut. That's first on the list as soon as I get out and get back to my crib. My shit is going to be super crispy since I purposely let it grow while in here.

Lunch was served. I honestly don't even remember what it was and didn't bother writing it down. I was too excited to get out and get a real meal. I think my first meal once I'm out is going to be the miso salmon and brown rice from Cheesecake Factory. Elizabeth put me on to that months ago and that's since been my go-to meal whenever I order from there.

While waiting for a CO to come and get me, I read a few of the stories in today's Capital:

The 23-year-old Navy Midshipmen Michael Wallace, who was accused of rape back in March 2018, was acquitted of all his charges. He's a highly accomplished young white male with privilege and an abundance of resources, so I'm not surprised to learn of this outcome.

Zion officially declared for NBA draft. I, along with any person who follows college or professional basketball, knew this would be the case. Can't wait to watch the young fella at the next level.

Luke Walton was hired by the Sacramento Kings after just being let go from the Lakers this past Friday. He hasn't proven himself as being the super stellar coach, so I didn't expect him to get a job so soon. We'll see how this decision plays out this upcoming season.

I saw that the Clippers beat the Warriors last night in game 2, 135-131, and that Boogie Cousins may have torn his quad. Damn, it's been one obstacle after another in regard to Boogie remaining healthy and being a viable option for Golden State. I hope he bounces back ASAP. The 76ers also beat the Nets.

Last, Russell Wilson, the QB for the Seahawks, just collected a major bag. He re-signed with the Seahawks for 4 years and $140 million, making him the highest paid player in the NFL. Congrats to him.

That's it. The CO just called me to be released. I'll be going through the release process, given back my clothes and property that I brought in with me, changing, signing my release documents and will then be free to go.

My stay in JRDC has finally come to an end. I thank God for His protection and His favor; for an incredible support system and ensuring that I still have a job and resources upon my return. And, although I was only here for a short stay, I'm beyond grateful that He did not allow this place to break my spirit. This system chews and discards so many of my kind once they're in its clutches. I'm just blessed to not be 1 of the many that this place has gotten the best of.

I'm finally up out this bitch!! Thank you, God, once more for seeing me through one of the most trying times in my life, and allowing me to make it out unscathed. Peace and Love always.

About the Author

Darren Smith is from the small town of Shady Side, MD., and has resided in several other areas throughout Anne Arundel County, MD. He is a class of 2005 graduate of Severn School in Severna Park, MD. He went on to earn his bachelor's degree in Psychology from Howard University in Washington, DC in 2009, and his Master's in Social Work from the University of Connecticut in 2013. He chose the social service/helping profession because it is a broad field that consists of numerous opportunities, yet still maintains the overall focus of aiding the most vulnerable populations.

He currently works for DC Child and Family Services Agency (CFSA), where, as a Performance Monitor, he focuses mainly on contract compliance, quality assurance, and ensuring that foster parents and service providers throughout the District of Columbia are consistently adhering to the required licensing and clearance regulations set forth by the city.

In his free time, he enjoys listening to music, watching movies, documentaries, reading, writing, and traveling. Over the past 2 years, he has proudly accomplished the goal of traveling to all 7 Wonders of the World

Darren would like to thank God, his family, and incredible support system for helping him through this difficult time in his life, as well as for the constant encouragement they provided to share this experience with the world.

CPSIA information can be obtained
at www.ICGtesting.com
Printed in the USA
LVHW030546180820
663484LV00005B/329